BILL BRAMAH'S ONTARIO

Bill Bramah

illustrations by
Jerry J. Preston

Cannon
Toronto

Cannon

Cannon Book Distribution Ltd.
25 Connell Court, Unit 2, Toronto, Ontario
Canada M8Z 1E8
(416) 252-5207

Canadian Cataloguing in Publication Data

Bramah, Bill, 1915-
Bill Bramah's Ontario

ISBN 0-9691210-3-2

1. Ontario — Biography — Anecdotes, facetiae, satire, etc.
2. Ontario — History, Local — Anecdotes, facetiae, satire, etc.   I. Title

FC3061.8.B73 1985   971.3'002   C85-099185-4
F1057.6.B73 1985

Printed and bound in Canada
First Printing — July 1985
Second Printing — October 1985
Third Printing — January 1986
Fourth Printing — June 1988
Fifth Printing — March 1989
Copyright © 1985 by Bill Bramah

No part of this book may be reproduced or transmitted in any form by any means, electronic or mechanical, including photocopying and recording, or by any information storage or retrieval system, without written permission from the publisher. Exception is given to reviewers who may quote brief passages for the printed or electronic media.

Cover photo: Bill Bramah and young friends at Ste. Marie among the Hurons.

Cover photo by Rosemary Gilbert

Jerry Preston has specially designed this image to combine Bill's hand and microphone with Ontario's emblem of the trillium.

Table of Contents

Introduction 6

Southwestern Ontario
Ontario's Main Street 9
Punkydoodles Corner 11
Garden of Weeds 12
Granny's Duvets 13
World's Champion Birdwatcher 14
Elora's Power Play 15
Old Buggies 16
The Donnellys Today 18
Sled Dogs 19
The Sky's the Limit 20
Ontario Peanuts 22
Turkey Talk 23
Fishing Village 24
Kipp's Garage 25
The Slow-Pokes 26
Blueberry Patches 28
Ides of March 29
Butler's Farm Animals 30
Cobblestone Houses 32
Tintinnabulator 33
Lombardo Legend 34
Talking Earth Pottery 36
Kissing Bridge 38
Youngest Postmaster 39
Backus Mill 41
First Oil Well 42
Old Streetcars 43
"Doc" McKibbin 45
Fall Fairs 46
Oldest Pilot 47
Forge and Anvil 49

Eastern and Central Ontario

Boldt Castle	51
Birdhouse City	53
The Philoxians	54
The Magnetic Hill	55
Windmill Man	56
Fence Viewers	58
Painting Priest	59
Cactus Grower	60
Rendezvous for Seniors	61
Rockhounds	62
Joey the Beaver	64
Holland Marsh	65
Esmond's Tea Room	66
Monastery Row	68
Ice Fishing	69
Pirate Ship	70
Dream Come True	72
Raising Crickets	73
Dollhouse Gallery	75
Mr. Kite	76
Ginseng Farm	78
19th Century Man	79
Last Duel Park	80
Herb Homestead	82
Clock Auction	83
Buggy Man	84
School Patrollers	86
World's Champion Songwriter	87
Taj Mahal	88
Toymaker	90
Little Red Schoolhouse	91
Peterborough Postcard Company	93
The Forgotten Chapel	94
Merry-Go-Round	95
Len Cullen — Dreamer	96
Barn-Raising	98

Muskoka and Southern Georgian Bay

Roughing It 100
Backstage at Ste. Marie 102
Birdman of Bala 103
Scoots 104
Canada's Purest Water 106
Cranberry Farm 107
Marine Railway 108
Magic of Muskoka 109
Red Baron 110
Bygone Days Farm 112
Old Organs 113
The Hidden Talents 114
Steamer Clarke 116
Severn Bird Farm 117
Missing the Boat 118
Two Turtles 120
Heat from Peat 121
Maple Syrup 122
Budd Watson Gallery 124
Bigwin Inn 126

Northern Ontario

Harry's Chateau 128
Bush Pilot 130
Canada's Coldest Spot 131
Staking a Claim 132
James Bay Frontier 134
Canada's Largest City 136
Old Mountie 137
Timmins-Greenland Games 138
Beardmore Relics 140
The Dionnes Today 142
Science North 144
Highway Book Store 146

How To Get There 147

Introduction

This book was written in restaurants, hotels, motels, truck stops and other assorted nooks and crannies around the province. The stories are mostly about the little places that dot the countryside and the people who live there.

To find them I've trudged through the bush on snowshoes near places with wondrous names like Cripple Creek and wandered in the beauty of autumn at High Falls. For some stories I've moseyed around the mosaic of the city to meet artists, artisans, stuntmen and kitemakers. For others I've gone up in old planes, acrobatic jets, gliders and balloons, or out on fishing boats and schooners and down 5,000 feet to see a vegetable garden grow in an abandoned mine. But mostly, the stories were just waiting at the end of a country road.

It all started about eight years ago when Global TV asked me to roam Ontario looking for what were roughly described as "human interest" items. None of us knew exactly what we were looking for. There was no set plan, no specific number of items per week or anything like that. There still isn't.

They got me a sporty little Mustang with "Bramah's Ontario" on it and let me loose. They were too smart to let me go by myself. They made my wife, Jenny, a production assistant. She's a farmer's daughter and knows a lot about nature and fall wheat and other such truly meaningful things in life. I grew up in the city and come in handy in heavy traffic.

We travel about 4,000 miles a month and have gone through a series of Mustangs. But we don't always rush it. Sometimes it might take us a day to drive a couple of hundred miles. If we see something like an old mill, a baby buffalo or a man making buggies we stop to take a look at it.

The stories crop up willy-nilly. A good percentage come from people we meet on the road who tell us about something interesting or unusual in their community.

Somewhere along the line I began to rewrite the stories for radio and for a few years did a daily stint on Toronto's CFRB radio station along with writing a newspaper column which still goes to a group of weeklies.

When one of the Global editors suggested a book I thought I'd give it a whirl. I'm glad I did. It's given a chance to renew acquaintance with the places, people, birds, animals and all the other things around the province I've come to know and love.

I hope you enjoy meeting them too.

Southwestern Ontario

Highway 401 in evening dress. (upper photo)
Highway 401 at work. (lower photo)
photo by: M. Light

Ontario's Main Street

When you've been on the road for awhile, the major highways seem to take on a character of sorts.

I've come to think of Highway 400 as a free spirit. It leads to Cottage Country. To Muskoka and Georgian Bay. It's the road to freedom.

Highway 403 is an adolescent. It hops from Highway 401 to the Queen Elizabeth Way. At Hamilton, it gets confused and finally decides to go in the general direction of Brantford. It's still growing and isn't quite sure of what it's supposed to do.

But Highway 401, the superhighway that slices across Southern Ontario from Windsor to Quebec is in a class by itself. It's in its middle years and has been through the mill. It's Ontario's Main Street. It's the workhorse. It's been kicked around. And it kicks back with traffic jams and pileups. It's been bruised and bent and has a few battlescars. But like an old pro, it's there in the clutch. And it has its pride. After all, it's famous!

Did you know that Highway 401 is thought to be the longest freeway in the world? Or that at Toronto's Bathurst Street, the highway's 16 lanes make it the widest in the world? Did you know that over 230,000 cars pass that area in a single day? These things make the 401 world class! A champion!

Orv Harron of the Ministry of Transportation and Communications watched the highway grow. He was a young officeboy when they started to build it in 1947.

Orv says that putting down the first 16-mile stretch from Oshawa to Scarborough was a real headache. Nobody wanted it. City people said it was useless, stuck "way up north". Farmers wielding pitchforks chased the first survey crews off their land!

It wasn't even called 401 until five years later when it had grown to what was considered a whopping 35 miles. But after 20 years and 425 million dollars, it had scooted 510 miles across the province.

"If this highway had been built in the United States," says Orv, "it would have been known throughout the world as an unsurpassed engineering marvel. It's probably broken all kinds of records. But we Canadians are very reserved about things like that."

January 4th is 401's unofficial birthday. I'm often taking one of my frequent jaunts along the superhighway when its anniversary rolls around. And I sometimes recall the many times my old friend has helped me out. I forget its temper tantrums and think about the hours it has saved me in travelling time.

But there isn't must point in wishing it a "Happy Birthday." After all, to the poor old 401, it's just another day to be banged, bashed, torn up, and run over.

I suppose that's part of the price of fame.

Punkydoodles Corners

Have you ever heard of Dog's Nest? How about Skunk's Misery or Punkydoodles Corners?

They're just a few of the little hamlets with strange names that pop up every once in a while when you're driving along country roads.

You chuckle when you spot the names. By the time you've finished the chuckle, you've left the place.

Dog's Nest is down on Lake Erie near Port Dover. Skunk's Misery is near London. Punkydoodles Corners is in the Kitchener-Waterloo-Stratford area. Somewhere in there.

I've been to Punkydoodles Corners twice. The first time I missed it completely. You've got to be quick. There are only three houses in Punkydoodles Corners and you can arrive and depart in just a few seconds.

Another difficulty is the lack of those blue signs the government puts up at the entrance of cities, towns, and villages.

There is no sign to let you know you're entering Punkydoodles Corners. They've tried putting them up. They've tried many times. But tourists can't resist the signs. They cart them off — mostly in the dead of night. One Punkydoodles Corners sign stayed up for a week. That was an all-time record!

The second time I visited Punkydoodles, I had no trouble finding it all all. Cars were parked all around the hamlet and spilled over down to the main highway! Thousands of people were there! It was a day in the early 80's when Punkydoodles Corners held its Canada Festival!

The tiny community is bordered by three counties, and the MPP's involved organized the event. There was a plowing match and booths and balloons and games and dancing and the whole affair was a huge success.

Politicians and media people swarmed all over. A cairn was erected commemorating the occasion. Best of all, Punkydoodles Corners had its own post office for the day! Canada Post set up a portable in an alfalfa field and issued a special stamp! To top it all off, a baby was born to one of the families that day, and the population soared to 14!

It seems there's always been a certain prestige in living in the hamlet, but after the Canada Festival, the people were fairly bursting with civic pride.

During the festivities, Harvey Mueller, a long-time resident told me that some farmers in the district brag they're from Punkydoodles Corners. But they're not.

Said Harvey, "They're usually trying to impress people. As far as we're concerned, they just live in the suburbs."

Garden of Weeds

Did you ever see a beautiful, cultivated garden of weeds? That's right — weeds!

Jack Alex has one, and he spends a lot of time caring for it. He puts pesticides and herbicides on it. He plants weed seed. He gives his weed garden tender loving care.

You can see the garden from a window of his third floor office at the University of Guelph. Dr. Alex is a botanist and hundreds of students, farmers and naturalists visit his garden of weeds every year.

Even in early autumn it's an impressive sight. There are 150 different varieties of weeds. They range from familiar types like wild mustard to the more exotic ones such as the flowering Jerusalem artichoke, the velvet leaf, and the deceiving poke weed which at first glance looks like a bush laden with grapes.

I learned that Goat's Beard is also called Johnny-go-to-bed-at-noon. It actually does close up shop late in the morning. Another attractive weed is Our Lady's Bedstraw, which was used for stuffing mattresses in pioneer days, and the Bouncingbet was used as a substitute for soap.

Dr. Alex has written a book called "Ontario's Weeds" which goes into detail on the nature of weed life. Apparently, you can get all sorts of books on the subject. And there's one with the somewhat adventurous, devil-may-care title, "Stalking the Wild Asparagus".

Dr. Alex goes in the opposite direction to most gardeners. Something like "Mary, Mary quite contrary".

And how does his garden grow? Well, before you know it, you begin to believe that weeds really are beautiful, as he literally leads you down the garden path.

Granny's Duvets

Ann Eckart makes duvets. Those cosy comforters with a solid country look. The kind Granny used to make. Granny knew what she was doing. She knew that the feathery down of geese is one of nature's wonder insulations.

Ann Eckart knows it too. She lives in the little village of Jerseyville in Southwestern Ontario. When she and her husband moved to their country home on the outskirts of the village, they decided to raise a few geese. The flock grew, and before long, they didn't know what to do with all the down they had.

"We put a little ad in the paper and the phone rang off the hook. We sold the down in no time. Some of the callers asked for duvets, and of course, I didn't have any," says Ann.

But it gave her an idea. In her native Holland, sewing is taught as early as Grade 1, and although she had been sewing for years, she had to learn the tricks of stitching and design needed to keep the light fluffy down inside the coverings. So she began adapting her knowledge to down.

It took only a few gifts to relatives to prove that she had a winner and she started selling the duvets she made. Then she turned to designing and making winter clothing for handicapped children.

"I saw a need for it," Ann says. "It's all made to measure and especially useful for those who have cerebral palsy or are confined to wheelchairs." She showed me how the special closures and designs made them easy to put on. The jackets especially, are very simple, but very ingenious.

As I mosey around the countryside, I learn all sorts of things you rarely learn at school. Ann was telling me that feathers haven't nearly the insulating qualities that down has.

She demonstrated with a gallon-sized glass bottle of pure down that was sitting on the huge table where Ann makes the duvets. She took off the top and I plunged my hand inside. Immediately, I felt heat. That was because the trapped air spaces were hanging on to the heat from my hand. That's the secret of down's warmth. It traps heat from the body.

The Eckarts have raised up to 350 geese to provide down for what's now called Downcraft Products. They need them. Ann sells duvets as fast as she can make them. And it takes 25 geese to produce 2 pounds of down — enough for one double-bed size duvet!

World's Champion Birdwatcher

A few years ago I went to Point Pelee for the spring migration and became a born-again bird-watcher! I'm still not sure how it happened. I'd always taken a lukewarm look at "birders". I always liked to think of myself as a detached philosopher about such matters.

That spring I changed. Maybe it was the atmosphere around Wigle's Motel in Leamington where birders meet year after year. Maybe it was Norman Chesterfield. I was there to do a story about him.

Norman is a well-to-do mink rancher who lives in the little fishing village of Wheatley, close to Point Pelee. But he's known by birders all over the world. He's in the Guiness Book of World Records. Because Norman Chesterfield is the world's champion birder!

I met him shortly after he had wrested the title from Stuart Keith of New York City. Keith had been the leader of the pack for years.

Norman turned out to be a deceiving guy. He appeared to be about 50, but was crowding 70 at the time. He was serene, mild-mannered, and didn't look like a go-getter at all. But underneath is a seething, competitive spirit. Anyway, that's what his wife Jean told me. He denied this. He said it wasn't a desire to be Number One that drove him. It was just a great interest in birds.

"Don't let him kid you," snapped Jean. "He's a fanatic about winning." I dropped the subject and asked him how he managed to reach the astounding record of sighting and listing 5,586 species of birds!

He said he'd been working on it for 25 years. He's bird-scanned all the oceans and all the continents except Antarctica. He's been to more than 140 countries looking for different birds.

He flies everywhere. He'll take off for places like Tibet to see a rare bird as fast as you can say Roger Tory Peterson. And it's a running gag among birders that Norman flies more than some of the birds.

As we watched and talked, I began to notice the other birders. When a new bird was sighted, word got around quickly. There would be whispers and small groups would merge toward the bird's location. I sensed the excitement. Somebody said there was a Wilson Warbler nearby. Norman spotted it, and handed me his binoculars. I managed to close in on it. It was beautiful!

I go back to Point Pelee every year now. I guess, like the birds, instinct guides me.

By the way, the last time I saw Norman, his list had grown to more than 6,000 species!

Elora's Power Play

You could be back in the days of Charles Dickens when you walk along Elora's Mill Street. You expect to see Oliver Twist or David Copperfield appear at any moment.

The restored shops that were built by Scottish stone masons in the 19th century have an Old World charm that enthralls visitors to the little village in the Guelph area.

At the bottom of Mill Street is the Elora Mill Inn. With its massive solid oak beams and open fireplaces, it exudes the quality of life of another era.

The Inn overlooks the famed Gorge of the Grand River which attracts over a million people a year who marvel at the beauty of the cascading torrents.

A century ago, the rapids of the river provided power for the grist mill. It was a bustling industry in the village. As modernization took over, the mill went into decline and the power was needed no longer.

But recently, the Grand went back to work. Crozier Taylor, an innkeeper of the old school, bought the renovated mill a few years ago, and with some government backing, began work on the first private power project of its kind in the province.

A mini-hydro system was constructed, using the river's power. The mill's old race and power wheels had gone, so a new race and flume were built and a specially designed generator and turbine installed.

The system will produce an average of 150 kilowatts a day. The Inn's average requirement is 100 kilowatts a day. The excess will be sold to Ontario Hydro and Crozier estimates that the small plant will pay for itself over a seven-year period.

We were there when the lights went on for the first time. It was quite an event. There was a big crowd. Pipers played. There was music and laughter in the gracious old dining room. The lights were steady and bright.

I went over to one of the windows and peered through one of the square panes. The waters of the river seemed to be tearing along faster than usual. Maybe it was just my imagination.

But I felt sure the Grand and its Gorge were happy to be back on the job. They roared their approval!

Old Buggies

You get the feeling you're living in another era when you spend a few hours with the diminishing breed of Old Order Mennonites. We went to the village of Newton, near Elmira, to visit a shop where three generations of a Mennonite family work from dawn to dusk making buggies.

There are only four buggy factories in Canada. All of them are in Ontario. The Newton Buggy Works, as it's called, is one of the larger operations, and is owned by the Yantzi family.

The elder Yantzi is Samuel. He's over 70 but looks younger. His son, Solomon, now runs the shop. And Solomon's son, Douglas, is an apprentice.

They follow the Amish tradition. They live in a world apart, and have no truck with technology. There's no electricity, telephone, automobile, radio or TV. They wear black and ordinarily shun publicity like the plague.

When we explained to Solomon that few people likely know that buggy factories even exist anymore, he agreed to let us shoot some film.

We watched the Yantzi family and their two part-time helpers making buggies from scratch. They were using basswood.

It was a slow process. No one seemed to rush. But there was no fooling around either. And no coffee breaks.

There was a paint shop behind the main building where young Douglas was painting a completed buggy. Solomon said it would sell for about $1,200. They build about 20 buggies a year at the shop. Most of them are ordered by people from around the district although there have been orders from as far away as Scotland.

At the turn of the century there were many who maintained that those "new fangled" automobiles would never replace the horse. Well, it didn't turn out that way.

Nevertheless, within a ten-mile radius of Newton there are at least 100 families who still travel by horse and buggy on a regular basis. But here's the surprising thing. Only about 50% of them are Mennonites. The others just happen to like buggies.

The horse and buggy is a common sight in Mennonite country. But not all of the buggies are made for Mennonites.
photo by: J. Bramah

The Donnellys Today

You may have heard of the "Black Donnellys." They were a notorious family who came from Ireland in the 1800's and settled in Lucan, a village in Southwestern Ontario.

These days, Lucan is a quiet, friendly little place that was chosen as the site for the International Plowing Match one year. In other words, highly reputable.

But in the days of the Donnellys, it was Canada's most lawless town. Mostly because of the Donnellys. They were violent, hard-drinking, fighting men who continued a feud with their neighbours that began in the Old Country. Eventually, they were blamed for every criminal act that occurred in Lucan whether they did it or not.

The Donnellys died as violently as they had lived. On the night of February 4, 1881, five members of the family were mutilated and murdered by a vigilante committee in one of the most brutal murders in the annals of Canadian crime.

The vigilante group was made up of 40 villagers. Apparently even the town constable was in on it. And there were charges that the parish priest was one of the organizers.

The murderers were brought to trial but never convicted. The gory story fascinated people for generations and several books were written about the "Black Donnellys" as one writer called them.

Until recently, the mere mention of the Donnellys' name was taboo around Lucan. There were many descendants of the vigilantes still there.

But a few years ago another hangover from the Donnelly era cropped up. The old Catholic Church the family had attended was slated for demolition. Some of the parishioners wanted to tear it down and build a new one. Others felt it was historic and should be preserved. Finally, after a lengthy squabble an advisory board voted 9 to 8 to demolish it. But at the last moment the Bishop of the diocese intervened and saved it.

I went down to the village and talked to a few people about the church. Some said it should have been destroyed, and with it, the memory of the Donnellys.

Others thought differently. One woman said, "It's a good thing they're keeping it. At one time almost everybody around here was hatched, matched and dispatched in that church."

Things have changed in Lucan. The old guard is dying out. The new families don't mind talking about the Donnellys at all.

You can even buy baseball caps and T-shirts emblazoned with "Lucan — Home of the Black Donnellys."

Sled Dogs

On one of those lazy, hazy hot summer days we went to Tom Soper's farm near Chesley to see his sled dogs.

Chesley is a pleasant little town south of Owen Sound. Tom was North America's only entry in the International Open Dog Sled Races in Switzerland a few years ago. He and his dogs have won all sorts of trophies. They've appeared in movies. They're well known in sled dog circles.

So is Tom's wife, Marian. She not only races, she takes care of Tom, their three teenaged daughters and helps care for about 50 husky dogs as well. Her regular job though, is handling the books for the family monument business.

It was a most unlikely situation. It would have seemed appropriate in winter, but it was about 90 in the shade, and there were Tom and Marian hitching up eight sled dogs to go for a workout.

The dogs could hardly wait. Jenny stood well back. I joined her. Cameraman Tim Moses set up his equipment near a bend in a wooded land that runs through the farm.

Tom hopped on the back of a three-wheeled trainer and they were off.

My recollection of what happened in the next few seconds is vague. The dogs and Tom seemed to whiz by. They disappeared around the bend.

Jenny and I went over to see the other dogs. Each dog had its own doghouse. They were barking their heads off. They wanted to get into the act.

We waited for about half an hour. Then suddenly the team came tearing toward us. In the distance, Tim appeared lugging his camera and tripod. As he came closer we could see the big grin on his face. He had the shots he wanted.

But the highlight of the day for me was meeting "Yukon," the lead dog. He was 11 at the time and Tom said he was still the strongest and smartest dog.

Even more surprising, we learned he was the father of all the other dogs in the team. The team that raced both in Switzerland, and down the country lane on that sweltering day.

The younger dogs looked tired. "Yukon" didn't.

The Sky's the Limit

Some years ago, I took my first flight in a balloon. It was near Aurora. The pilot was Karen Rosenthal, Canada's first woman balloonist.

At that time, ballooning was just a hobby with her. But these days, Karen is a partner in a firm that makes hot air balloons. Her partner is Wayne Metler, one of only six balloon makers in the world!

I went to see them making the huge balloons at what they call "Fantasy Sky Promotions," in the village of Doon, on the outskirts of Kitchener.

It doesn't take long to get caught up in the romance of the sport. The balloons they make have exotic names like "Drifting Peace" and "Fantasy Seven" and if you've ever seen groups of them up in the air you know how they lend an aura of magic to the sky.

Making a balloon appears to be simple. But it's tricky. Wayne has been doing it for over a decade. He showed me a few of his designs and how the contours of the nylon envelope are precision-cut. The panels are sewn together, burners made for the propane heat that inflates the balloon, and Wayne's brother Lonnie weaves wicker into baskets called gondolas.

Karen's job is mainly to give demonstrations of the aircraft and give lessons, although she often helps with the designs.

As we recalled the time we took off into the sky at sunrise, she mentioned that the sport has mushroomed since the days when she was Canada's only woman balloonist.

"Ten years ago," she said, "there were only 5 balloonists in the whole country. Now there are 150 with licences, and 6 of them are women."

Wayne and Karen do their own testing. The standards for the balloons are the same as any other aircraft manufacturer, and as Wayne points out, ballooning has a lower accident record than any other type of aircraft.

As I left, I was thinking that aside from balloons, I've been up in gliders, acrobatic jets, bush planes and restored fighter planes from two World Wars. And one of those old planes was piloted by a skilled, vibrant ninety-year-old!

Dangerous? Not really. I felt far safer flying in any of them than I feel driving along my helpful, convenient but treacherous old buddy, Highway 401.

Ontario Peanuts

Farmers are great gamblers and they play for keeps. Nothing as simple as the roll of the dice. They don't just put money on the line. They put blood, sweat and tears into one of the riskiest, toughest, most thankless, but most important jobs in the world.

Sometimes the odds look pretty good. They looked good to Jim Picard in the late 70's. A successful farmer who had been growing corn down around Simcoe for years, he decided to take a run at growing peanuts.

Today, Picard Peanuts is a going concern. And quite a tourist attraction. Many of us have never seen a peanut processing plant and Jim has built a beauty. It's a big, blue structure that stands out on the skyline a few miles north of Simcoe.

Busloads of seniors and schoolchildren pull in and out periodically. Casual visitors come in, look around and while wandering about, gobble up "Little Goobers," as the peanuts are called commercially.

It's quite a set-up. But it didn't spring up overnight. There was a lot of study, a lot of planning, and a lot of selling to do. Jim travelled for months through peanut country in the States. He consulted farmers and agricultural experts. He investigated different types of equipment. It took a few years to collect the necessary data.

Then he began selling the notion. He managed to get the government interested and a few farmers in Southwestern Ontario liked the idea. The timing was right. Tobacco farmers were looking for supplementary crops, and the sandy soil was ideal. The first crop was planted in 1980.

That spring, I met Jim at his fledgling plant. He was enthusiastic about a new type of harvester he had. The building was up but there was very little equipment in it.

I returned for the harvest. Although some people may think so, the peanut, like money, doesn't grow on trees. It grows under the ground. That September I pulled up some of Canada's first peanuts. Global cameraman Vince Robinet got the shots, and since then we've been going back for the harvest year after year. Over 500 acres is now under cultivation by Jim and other farmers in the area.

There's always something new being added to the plant. It can now shell 30 tons of peanuts a day, and visitors can see them being graded, cooked, cooled and packaged.

There's also a small retail outlet at the front of the building where you can get peanut butter and extra packages of fresh "Little Goobers." And, of course, when you pick up a peck of Picard Peanuts, you're picking up a product from Ontario farmers' fields.

Turkey Talk

No matter how big the turkey was you ever had over any holiday season, it's unlikely it was anywhere near the size of the whoppers they raise at Hybrid Turkeys in the Kitchener area.

Hybrid is a big outfit. They have numerous farms and ship about half a billion little turkeys a year to 44 countries of the world.

But they also have a genetic division where they breed huge turkeys — some of them weighing up to 70 pounds! The world record is 78 pounds.

Mind you, that's out of a 3,000 gene pool. The 70-pound turkey is still a rare bird. It takes about a year for them to grow and by that time they're tough and stringy, but processors gobble them up for burgers and steaks.

I spent a day with Len Weaden, the firm's production manager, roaming around a few of the farms they have. They keep the big fellas at a farm near the village of New Dundee. There are about 100 of them fenced off in a large pen. Pound for pound, they're a match for a 10-year-old boy.

I discovered that when you try to talk turkey, the turkeys do all the talking. As soon as Len and I would begin to discuss something, the turkeys would interrupt. They'd begin to "gobble gobble" in unison at the sound of our voices. We finally had to go outside to talk.

Later on, we went to the company's offices in Kitchener and I saw scientists at work in a laboratory. They were telling me that in the future the 100-pound turkey is a possibility. If that happened you'd have a turkey big enough to feed a family reunion of 180 people!

Fishing Village

With its snug harbour and lighthouse on the pier, the fishing village of Port Dover is one of the most picturesque places in the province. There's none of that fancy window dressing you sometimes run into. No phony commercialism. It's the real thing!

We like to watch the fishing boats coming and going, walk out along the pier to visit the craft shops and fish stores. We watch the activity around Misiner's big fish processing plant, see the gulls soaring into the sky as Lake Erie's waves break against the shoreline.

We always stay at the Erie Beach Motel. Since we return time and again to various country inns and motels as we travel the province, the innkeepers and their staff get to know us. We even have our "own rooms." At the Erie Beach, owners Harold and Tony Schneider and executive secretary Ruth Bridgewater always book Jenny and I into Room 3 so we can get a good view of the lighthouse. Our regular waitress Laverne never asks us what we want at the restaurant. In Dover, we always get a "perch dinner." It's become traditional. Sometimes we go to Fred Knechtel's or Mike's Place for "perch and chips."

We've done quite a few stories around Port Dover. Stan Morris, editor of the "Port Dover News," gives us good leads. So do some of the people we meet on the main street or out on the pier.

We've made a number of friends in the village over the years. One of them is Elsie Murphy, a crusty newspaper columnist who has lived in Dover all her life. Elsie is a newshawk of the old school. In 30 seconds, she'll drawl out five good leads within a 20-mile radius. When we first met her, she mentioned that Ivey's Greenhouses might make a good yarn. I couldn't visualize it as particularly interesting when we had things like the Lighthouse Theatre Festival, teeming with interesting people. Or the Fishermen's Weekends. That's when all the Lake Erie fishermen come over to Dover and have tug pulls, and finally blow their stacks.

I let the greenhouse idea simmer for about four years and every once in awhile Elsie would remind me about it.

Finally, I went out to Ivey's just to get Elsie off my back. I expected to see a few pleasant gardeners clipping roses in a couple of hothouses. I should have known better.

I was astounded! There were roses everywhere. As far as you could see! I discovered that Ivey's Inc. grows four million roses a year! They employ about 200 people and have seven acres of greenhouses jammed close together. The company has been operating for over 75 years and the great-grandsons of the founder are now in the business.

I didn't waste any time getting the story done. And since then, I have always paid very close attention to what Elsie Murphy says.

Kipp's Garage

If you happen to be in the Southwestern Ontario town of Aylmer, take a look at Jerry Kipp's garage. Ask anybody where he lives — everybody knows, because the garage has become quite famous. It's made of orange juice bottles!

Here's what happened. During his days as a milkman, Jerry used to mystify his customers with the request that they save their orange juice bottles for him. They did, and he built up a collection of more than 3,000 bottles.

At that time he had an idea that he'd build a greenhouse with them. Then five years ago he started to build a garage on to his home. But he ran out of money half way through the job. He was stuck with a half-finished garage.

Then he thought of the bottles! He cemented them with mortar and glue and used them to complete the project. The neighbours were impressed. One of them suggested that Jerry submit his idea, along with a picture of the garage, to "Mechanics Illustrated", a magazine mostly for do-it-yourself types. The magazine has what they call The Golden Hammer — an award for new or ingenious ideas.

Jerry took their advice and was one of the three finalists. He lost out by a whisker to a fellow who built a new kind of solar home. But Jerry thinks he may have a winner with his next notion. He has lots of orange juice bottles left, so he's going to build an indoor swimming pool!

By the way, you'd never know the garage is made of juice jars — it looks more like glass brick. And it's practical. The air in the bottles acts as an insulator making it as good as a thermal pane.

Jerry's not sure how long it will take to build the swimming pool, but it's a pretty good bet he'll win The Golden Hammer this time for sure!

The Slow-Pokes

For years, I've been threatening to walk the Bruce Trail. The whole 438 miles of it along the edge of the Niagara Escarpment from Queenston to Tobermory, at the tip of the Bruce Peninsula on Georgian Bay.

I like to imagine myself as one of those hardy hikers who stride along with a packsack, camp overnight, and who are up at daybreak ready to cover another 20 miles or so.

I often get these vigorous, fit-as-a-fiddle spells while dawdling over my morning coffee in a comfortable hotel room. Preferably a woodsy place with open fireplaces and an efficient room service.

I hesitate to fulfill this dream of high adventure because the rapid pace of the hikers I have seen doesn't seem to fit into my way of life.

That's why I was so interested in meeting the Slow-Poke Hikers. They're a group in their Golden Years who live around the Golden Horseshoe area and have a different approach to hiking.

I guess you could call it a non-aggressive approach. They mosey along. They stop to smell the daisies. They'll pause to admire a walking fern. They'll take time to follow a bee through the sun-dappled forest to his honey tree. They'll follow the soaring wheeling rhythm of a turkey vulture as it picks up air currents.

There are about 20 Slow-Pokes and they talk a lot while they walk. It's mostly friendly banter. They clown around. They chuckle about

Bill, Vic and Elsie (at right) listening as some of the slow-pokes tell of their experiences on the Bruce Trail.
photo by: P. Materiuk

the distance they've covered. When I saw them in action, it had taken them seven years to cover just 120 miles of the Trail!

The founder of the Slow-Pokes is Vic Franklin, a veteran hiker in his seventies who lives in the village of Burford. As he grew older, he got fed up with the do-or-die method of conquering the Bruce. So he advertised for hikers who wanted to loaf along the Trail with him.

The first to answer the ad was my friend Elsie Murphy, crusty columnist for a weekly paper down Lake Erie way. Elsie started beating the drum and before long they had an enthusiastic group of followers. Enthusiastic with certain reservations.

Every spring they'd get out and do their bit on the Trail, as other clubs do, clearing away winter's debris. They'd meet once a week. They still do.

I met them one morning as their cars nosed in to Vic's backyard and they scrambled out. Admittedly, a sort of slow scramble. Their greetings were uproarious as if they hadn't seen each other for months.

They welcomed me warmly and off we went. Shuffling along. We didn't hike very far, but as the conversation drifted to walking the Bruce end to end, I felt another spell coming on. A vibrant, healthy, fit feeling. I had a vision. All of us were arriving triumphant at Tobermory.

I often think of the Slow-Pokes. Maybe someday I'll join them. Come to think of it, with my track record, I'd probably slow them down.

Blueberry Patches

I like blueberries. I've liked them since I was a lttle kid and used to pick them from low bushes when my family would take me on trips up around the islands of Georgian Bay. I like them better than strawberries, raspberries or blackberries. I know that's a pretty sweeping statement, but that's the way it is.

As I grew older and didn't have as much time to dawdle along picking blueberries, I'd buy them from fruit stores. But mostly, as I recall, they were imported from Michigan. I used to wonder why somebody didn't go into the blueberry business in Ontario. Well, about a decade ago a few people did. And now, there are close to 30 commercial highbush blueberry patches in the province.

The biggest one is Blue Ridge Farms at St. Williams on Lake Erie's north shore. It's run by Martin and Margo Weber, a couple of go-getters who sunk their savings into some of the sandy soil of Southwestern Ontario and haven't had to sing the blues since they started.

Blue Ridge has 20,000 bushes that seem to extend as far as the eye can see. From the middle of July till the end of the season, people are coming and going all the time. They can either buy boxes or baskets of berries from a stand at the entrance to the farm, or go out and pick their own.

The last time I was there they had a fancy new sprayer and were building a massive harvester which will rumble along and pick hundreds of the big blueberries in one fell swoop.

Needless to say when I'm let loose among those berries I'm a goner for a couple of hours. I think I eat as much as I pick. A few more customers like myself and Blue Ridge would rapidly become a non-profit organization.

Of course, there are several similarly excellent farms around these days. I've visited just a few of them. Diana Parks has a big one in the Thamesville area and near the town of Simcoe, there's a smaller but very lively spread called "Powell's Patch." It's operated by entrepreneur Chuck Powell who uses a number of germicides to keep hungry birds from the berries. Chuck has ferocious-looking stuffed owls set up on poles to frighten off the birds. He also has a small cannon that goes off every once in a while, and occasionally he wanders through the patch and imitates the cry of the dreaded red-tailed hawk.

But he says the most effective measure is provided by good old rock'n'roll! Chuck has a speaker secreted under the hood of his panel truck. When he drives the truck around the patch the rock music that blares out scares the bejeebers out of the birds! And if that doesn't work, he switches over to rhythm and ... uh, blues.

The Ides of March

In the Roman calendar, March 15th was known as the "Ides of March." It was an unlucky day like Friday the 13th.

In Shakespeare's play "Julius Ceasar," a soothsayer, a kind of prophet, warned Caesar to "beware the Ides of March." Caesar ignored the warning. But it was the day he was assassinated.

Here's the connection. One March 15th, I went down to the Stratford Festival Theatre to do a story about the Ides of March. I wrote a skit which involved Jack Medley who was to play Caesar that year, Mervin "Butch" Blake who was the soothsayer, and myself as Cassius, the villain of the play.

Since it was March 15th, the director didn't want us to do it. He said it would be unlucky. A theatre superstition.

But we talked him out of it, went ahead with the skit and filmed it. It turned out well and we ran it on Global News. Then we forgot about it.

But later, things began to happen. In one of the final rehearsals, Jack Medley's protective covering slipped and during the assassination scene he was accidentally stabbed.

He spent six weeks in hospital and had to be replaced by his understudy in the play, James Bradford.

When he was released from hospital, he began rehearsals for another play but was stricken by an intestinal problem. He required two operations.

All this led me to return to Stratford later to enquire further about superstitions in the theatre.

I talked to both "Butch" Blake and James Bradford. Blake is a veteran actor and told me about several theatre superstitions.

The one I found most interesting was about Shakespeare's "Macbeth." Theatre people consider it unlucky even to mention the name. Actors refer to it as "that Scottish play." It seems that something always happens to actors who play in "Macbeth."

And did the fact that we did our skit on March 15th have anything to do with Jack Medley's bad luck?

Nobody would give me a straight answer. But it's a safe bet to say that no director will let me near the Stratford stage again on the Ides of March!

Butler's Farm Animals

There's a beautiful farm on the outskirts of the Southwestern Ontario city of Woodstock, with a big white farmhouse that overlooks a most unusual barn.

The barn is chock full of animals. Nothing too unusual about that, except they're all on canvas. The barn is an art gallery jammed with what are some of the world's best known paintings of domestic animals.

The artist is Ross Butler. He's crowding 80, but has the same enthusiasm for his work as he likely had when, as a boy of seven, he began drawing the animals that roamed his father's farm in the nearby village of Norwich.

Visitors to the Butler gallery gasp when they walk in and see the variety of the paintings, and especially the one of the Holstein cow they remember seeing when they were schoolchildren.

In the late thirties, that cow made Butler famous. It was the True Type Holstein commissioned by the Holstein Association. The idea was to show the ideal Holstein — something breeders could work toward.

There were literally millions of prints and models of the cow sent around the world. A million or more were sent to Canadian schools alone.

Scattered around the gallery are paintings of horses, poultry and all sorts of domestic animals that illustrate Butler's meticulous artistry.

The most spectacular single work is a huge painting of every farm animal you can think of. It shows cows, sheep, swine and chickens moving from a farmyard to a fair, and finally to the Coliseum at the C.N.E.

The original painting took a full year to complete and Ross estimates that he touched the big canvas with paint more than 300,000 times before the work was finished.

Another of Butler's classics is called "Winners at the Royal." A typical Oxford County farm landscape forms the background for nine magnificent Holsteins, all of them the finest of the breed.

Ross Butler has had all sorts of honours heaped upon him. But it wasn't always that way. During the Great Depression, he'd sell a painting for a meal or a pair of pants.

These days he can write his own ticket and paints when he feels like it. One of his big joys in life is showing visitors around his gallery.

He's a farm boy who went to the top — in his own well-cultivated field.

Ross Butler, Bill and "Winners at The Royal". It's the artist's favourite painting.
photo by: T. Culbert

Cobblestone Houses

The last time I saw Paris was about 30 years ago. That's not the Gay Paree of the Eiffel Tower and the Sorbonne I'm talking about. It's Paris, Ontario. Population 7,500.

Paris is a pretty town at the "Forks of the Grand," as the brochures say. It has an attractive old world look.

I used to visit it once a week to gather news for the nearby Brantford radio station where I was a newscaster for a time.

I always enjoyed my weekly trips to Paris. But I was looking in the wrong direction for news. Young and bushy-tailed, I was chasing fire engines instead of looking at the town's architecture. As a result, I didn't find out until recently that Paris has more cobblestone buildings than any other place in Canada!

There are 12 of them and all but one were built by the same man. He was a master mason named Levi Boughton who lived in Paris during the last century.

Margaret Deans of the Paris Heritage Committee sent me some material about the cobblestone houses, along with a picture of one of the churches and I went down to take a look at them.

I met Margaret at a little restaurant called "The Coffee Cup" on the main street. Bill Gilchrist, at that time editor of the "Paris Star," the town's weekly newspaper, joined us briefly. It was press day and he had to keep moving. I understood perfectly. Contrary to popular opinion, weekly editors are usually a lot busier than editors of metropolitan dailies.

After that, Margaret took me on a tour of the town. The first stop was St. James Anglican Church. It was the first cobblestone structure Levi Boughton built in the town. That was in 1839. Then we went to a beautiful old cobblestone house where Alexander Graham Bell lived for awhile.

We saw a few more of the houses as well as Paris Plains Church. That's the only one that Boughton didn't build. It was constructed by pioneers of stones gathered from their own farms.

Finally, we went to the Deans' own cobblestone house. I met Margaret's husband Bill, and their three children. Bill's family have lived in the big home for five generations.

Bill was telling me that what you actually see of the cobblestones is just the tip of iceberg. He showed me a typical cobblestone. It was heavy and about eight inches long. The stones are set in an oblong fashion and all you see is a few inches of the stone. Behind the stones is about a foot of rubblestone. These houses were built to last!

As a parting shot, I learned that Plaster of Paris got its name from Paris, Ontario. The first plaster came from the limestone of the Grand River!

The Tintinnabulator

Ever hear of a tintinnabulator? They're a rare breed. There's only one in Ontario and he works out of his home in Waterdown, a little town near Burlington.

A tintinnabulator is a craftsman who sells, installs and repairs church bells. And Ontario's only tintinnabulator is Art Scott who's been in business for 50 years.

To be in this unusual game you have to have some unusual qualifications. First of all you have to have an exceptional musical ear. You must also have a mechanical aptitude. And these days, you must know something about electronics.

Art has all of these qualifications. His ears don't have a trace of tin in them. Fooling around with mechanical things doesn't phase him a bit and he's been in electronics since the early days of radio.

He lives in a world of bells. When you walk into his workshop and studio you're surrounded by them. There are clay bells, sleigh bells, ship bells, all kinds of bells he's collected over the years.

Scott was telling me that electronics changed the art of bell making. Through the use of amplifiers a miniature bell can produce the same volume as a four-ton giant of a bell.

Currently, Art is constantly travelling around the province installing electronic bells or repairing old church bells. But he can't find anyone to train to succeed him. Those triple-threat qualifications for being a tintinnabulor make it tough to find a candidate.

Art has no intention of retiring at the moment. And he'd better not. Not until he finds a replacement, anyway. With all the church bells scattered all over the province we need at least one tintinnabulator!

The Lombardo Legend

I spent an Auld Lang Syne day in London. It was mid-winter and New Year's Eve had come and gone. But when I walked into the Guy Lombardo Museum, a huge photo of Guy and his brothers greeted me, the smooth sound of saxophones glided from out of nowhere and waves of nostalgia swept me back to another era.

Guy Lombardo and the Royal Canadians — as a Cleveland promoter suggested they call themselves — were possibly the best known of all the big bands of yesteryear.

One reason was their New Year's Eve broadcasts from New York's Hotel Roosevelt, which were tied in to the mammoth celebrations in Times Square. Listening to the show on network radio, and in later years seeing it all on television, became an annual tradition for millions of people.

Guy, and brothers Carmen, Victor and Liebert, were born in London. As children, they took music lessons from an elderly musician named Professor Venuta whose studio was near Beal Technical School as I recall.

In their early teens, the boys formed a quartet and played around the area for dances. In the '20's, Guy expanded the band and developed the simple, melodic style which brought fame and fortune. By the early '70's, the band had sold 300 million records!

The Lombardos returned to London several times to renew old acquaintances and play at special functions. Nor did London forget its favourite sons. Out on Springbank Road is "The Guy Lombardo Bridge" and the Lombardo Museum is set among the trees a few hundred yards away near the banks of the Thames River.

It contains artifacts such as Guy's violin and baton, his familiar red jacket and memorabilia in the form of letters and plaques that were given to him by everyone from Presidents to the Sons of Italy. Dominating the small museum is Tempo VII, one of Guy's speedboats. At one time or another, Lombardo held nearly every U.S. record for powerboats.

Later in the day, we went down to Port Stanley, a picturesque fishing village and holiday resort on Lake Erie. We saw the Lombardo family's former summer home and the site of the old Stork Club. Before it was destroyed by fire, it was considered Canada's largest dance hall. Almost all of the big bands played there, including the Royal Canadians.

It brought back a lot of memories. I edited the village's first newspaper in the late '30's and interviewed Guy one time when the band was doing a one-night stand.

Should Guy Lombardo be forgotten? Not as far as the people in the London area are concerned. At the Museum, the Lombardo legend lives on.

The Lombardo brothers in their heyday. In London the legend lives on.

Talking Earth Pottery

There's a wealth of wisdom in the heritage of our native people. If you keep your eyes, ears and mind open some of it may rub off. But you have to keep your heart open to really feel it.

Sometimes I sense it from the Indian people I've met along the way. I was really aware of it when we met Steve Smith, a ruggedly handsome man and his beautiful wife, Leigh.

They have a place called "Talking Earth Pottery." It's on Sourspring Road which runs through the Six Nations Reserve near Brantford.

They work in a snug log cabin set back a few hundred yards from the road. It's tucked away in a forest of tall birch, maple and poplar.

Sunbeams were streaming through the small windows. They bounced back from pieces of pottery on shelves around the room. Beautiful pottery with the 'smokey' look that characterized the work of the Mohawks centuries ago.

Pottery made with turtles, bears and butterflies painted with

loving artistry on the bowls, vases and plates. Pottery such as we had never seen before.

The figures are all symbolic. The Smiths have never veered from their traditional beliefs. They retain a keen awareness of the order of nature.

I became absorbed in a bowl shaped like a turtle. It was divided into four parts representing health, life, growth and fertility. To the Indian, the turtle symbolizes the North American continent. You could spend years studying the mythology. Indians call it "spirituality." Many still live it. Others have been torn away from it to their sorrow and our loss.

We first met the Smiths in the '70's. At that time, Steve was doing odd jobs and Leigh was driving a school bus. They worked on the pottery when they had some spare time.

They had become devoted to the craft but couldn't make a living at it. At one point, they just about gave up. But they found they couldn't. They experimented. They worked up to 16 hours a day on it. Gradually, they found the germ of what they were looking for. Gradually, they developed the craft into an art. People heard about them and began to seek out their cabin.

Today, upstairs in the cabin, the walls are lined with pictures of world famous people being presented with "Talking Earth" pottery, presents from the governments as something truly representative of Canada's origins.

Ordinarily, I like to stay on the move. But as we pulled out and headed back to Highway 401, I didn't want to say goodbye. Didn't want to shed the serenity the Smiths had brought us for a few brief hours.

I also knew our paths would cross again.

Kissing Bridge

One day when I was in Mennonite Country, around Elmira, I took a short run over to West Montrose — a beautiful little village that's the home of The Kissing Bridge.

The Kissing Bridge is something of a tourist attraction. It's the only remaining covered bridge in Ontario. It's not a big bridge. It's about 200 feet long. But it's that wooden roof and siding that gets people — especially historians. And lovers!

The roof was designed to keep the snow off the bridge, but in the old days it provided couples with a certain privacy. That's how it became known as The Kissing Bridge.

There's a plaque beside the entrance giving a few details of the bridge's history. A builder named John Bear and his sons worked on it for more than a year, and charged $3,000 for the job. That was considered a fair price in 1881.

Young couples out for a buggy ride or a stroll along the banks of the Grand River began to catch on to the bridge. The Township fathers finally had a meeting and decided they'd better install a light. So they put up a lantern. But I guess they'd been young once themselves, and it wasn't much of a lantern. So the bridge remained sufficiently dingy to be appealing. These days there are electric light bulbs in it, but they're not very strong. It's still dingy.

From a practical point of view the bridge is withstanding the test of time. It's still the only way to cross the Grand River. From a romantic point of view you'd think that it would have outlived its usefulness. But the villagers at the general store were telling me that couples (mostly tourists of course) still use The Kissing Bridge. It's traditional. And some couples always visit it on their wedding anniversaries.

Youngest Postmaster

People seem to grouch about the weather more than any other single item on life's agenda, but possibly the post office runs a close second.

We're inclined to think of the post office as a huge bureaucracy that lumbers along at a snail's pace. We tend to believe that it should be run with the same faultless efficiency that we run our own lives. And it likely is. That's part of the problem.

But every once in a while, something happens to disturb all the prejudices we've built up so carefully over the years.

One beautiful autumn day I was driving through the countryside in Southwestern Ontario. I was thinking what a wonderful harvest we were having and my mind wandered to poetic thoughts about nature and the fruits of the land.

While in this poetic frame of mind, I lost my way on the country roads and ended up in a little village called Harley, somewhere south of Brantford. I was looking for a farm in the district where I was to do a story. I checked at the General Store. They didn't know where it was. They suggested the post office.

Harley isn't very big but I had a hard time finding the post office. It was camouflaged behind some old oak trees. I went into the place expecting the ultimate in inefficiency.

Inside, behind a small postal wicket was a young man I thought might be a high school student who worked there part-time. He was a nice, clean-cut kid wearing a jogging outfit and a baseball cap.

"Can I help you sir?" he said with a big smile and a slow drawl. I was no longer in a poetic mood. I was late and didn't have time to fool around.

"Could I see the postmaster," I said somewhat impatiently.

"I am the postmaster," he said, "I'm Shannon Good and this is my sister Rhonda." He nodded over to a young girl sorting mail. "And over there is Grandpa. He's 79 but still delivers our mail every day."

I was slightly stunned. I figured I must be talking to the youngest postmaster and the oldest carrier in the country.

It turned out that Shannon was 22 years old at the time, and became the postmaster when he was 20, succeeding his mother who was transferred to a nearby village.

I told Shannon my problem. He knew the farm I was trying to locate. He dropped everything. Leaving Grandpa in charge, he hopped in to his car and led the way to my destination about 10 miles away. I arrived on time.

As he drove off, waving goodbye, I vowed no matter what happened, I'd never, ever complain about the postal service again!

Backus Mill at Port Rowan. It survives today because of a clever ruse well over a century ago.
photo by: M. Light

Backus Mill

Every once in awhile John Backus goes over to visit the house where he was born and roams around the area where his family settled in 1792. John now lives in Port Rowan on Lake Erie, just a couple of miles away from the big homestead, the saw mill, the gristmill he used to operate, the creek, the forest and what's now called The Backus Conservation Area.

Sometimes John is called upon to don a top hat and frock coat, and impersonate his great-great-great grandfather! That's for special events.

The first John Backus was an enterprising settler and conservationist. The Backus Woods, all 600 acres of it, is still the only forest of its kind in the province where you can see such a variety of trees. There are trees you may have never seen before like sassafrac, cucumber, coffee, walnut and Florida dogwood. Trees of great age and size and species that are found nowhere else in Ontario.

But it's the Backus grist mill that historians drool over. Old John built it in 1798. That makes it Ontario's oldest mill and the oldest in the country to be operated continuously by one family.

Ordinarily John doesn't bother going to the mill during the winter. He's over 70 and has a lot of hobbies to take care of. But his boyhood friend, historian Harry Barratt, who lives in nearby Port Dover, persuaded him to show me around.

John ran the grist-mill as a commercial venture until about 20 years ago when the family sold it to the Black Creek Conservation Authority. It's a picturesque place with hand-hewn beams, wooden pegs instead of nails and a restored water wheel. The mill wasn't operating when we were there because the creek was frozen over. But in the summertime it goes full tilt so people can see how things were done in the old days.

Every schoolchild in the district knows about the mill's great moment in history. It happened during the war of 1812. The Americans burned all the mills along Lake Erie's shores. But the Backus mill was saved by a clever ruse. One of the family got the bright idea of setting fire to a big pile of straw a short distance from the mill. From a distance it appeared to the enemy that the mill was on fire and it wasn't until they had pulled out that they learned they had been tricked. To the Americans that was the last straw! They never returned.

By the way, the sign outside the old mill spells the family name as "Backhouse". That was the original name, but old John's wife considered it indelicate. John didn't want to change it. She insisted and finally he gave in and switched to Backus.

All the schoolchildren know that story too!

First Oil Well

When you tell people that the world's first oil well was drilled at Oil Springs, near Sarnia, they generally do a double take! And when you tell them that the continent's first oil family still lives there, they figure it's a gag of some sort and wait for the punchline.

It was news to me too until a few years ago when I met Charlie Whipp, a former newspaperman who was beating the drum for a museum called "The Petrolia Discovery," which portrays the history of oil in that area.

Whipp took me over to meet Charles Fairbank Jr., whose great great grandfather, J.H. Fairbank, drilled his first well in Oil Springs in 1861. While other pioneers left for foreign lands — Venezuela, the Mid-East and Russia — to show the world how to drill for oil, "J.H." stayed around. He built up a business that was to combine oil production and refining, farming, blacksmithing, banking and a hardware business.

I dropped in to say hello to "Young Charlie", as he's known around Petrolia and Oil Springs. He's now in his forties and was a high school teacher until oil hit the headlines. He left teaching and came home to run the family oil fields. They still exist. There are 140 wells and they turn out top quality crude. But here's the surprising thing — the oil is brought to the surface by a pumping system that "J.H." invented 120 years ago!

It's a "jerker-rod" system that allows you to drive scores of wells from one power source. Mind you, the wells produce only about 50 barrels a day — a trickle compared to the big companies. But engineers are amazed when they see those 19th century pumps bobbing up and down and oil bubbling out.

Charles considered modernizing the fields, but decided against it. As it stands, he can operate the Fairbank Oil fields with just four men and they're showing a tidy profit. As Charles puts it, "why change? The thing works!"

Old Streetcars

The Halton Country Radial Railway isn't very big. There's only one mile of track. But the track follows a wonderfully scenic route that runs through a woods near the village of Rockwood in the Guelph district. And the cars that travel it are ancient streetcars.

We went out to see the railway in action. We arrived at a little old-fashioned station just in time to see old 1326 rounding the bend.

It's a trolley that used to rush along Toronto's bustling Bay Street in the early Thirties. Now it casually rambles through the beautiful woodlands leading to the station.

There was the clang of a bell, the motorman brought her into the station, jumped down and came over to greet us.

His name was Lorne Hymers and he looked just like one of the older T.T.C. motormen I remember from when I was a child.

Lorne is one of the group of streetcar enthusiasts who, over the 20 years, have lovingly restored 14 of the venerable electric cars, returning them to the tracks so that visitors can get a glimpse of our trolley transportation history.

Many of the people who keep the trolley museum going are retired T.T.C. employees. But others, like Bob Johns, are still in the business.

Bob used to be with the T.T.C.; now he works with GO trains. In his spare time, he goes out to the museum to work on the old street cars.

When I suggested it must be sort of a busman's holiday, he said, "Not at all. It's a totally different dimension. There's a lot of history packed into the cars. People like to look at them, ride them and the kids just love them. That makes it all worthwhile."

The museum has more than just T.T.C. cars. Number 107, with its stained glass windows and polished maple interior, is from Montreal. And Number 8 is a 1915 model that ran on the London and Port Stanley Railway.

But the pride of the fleet is open-air Car 327. It has a running board along the side and was in use from 1890 to 1915.

Lorne gave us a ride on it. We went a heady 15 miles an hour. It wasn't a long journey. Just the mile of track, but a track that took us on a trip back in time. Like the kids, we loved it!

"Doc" McKibbon and one of his many patients. His methods are unusual, the results phenomenal.
photo by: V. Robinet

"Doc" McKibbin

It's been said that Dr. Lloyd McKibbin is a godsend to horsemen, a gadfly to other veterinarians.

When I visited him at his place on the outskirts of Wheatley, a village in Southwestern Ontario, the controversial vet was treating a sleek pacer's foreleg with a laser beam — of all things!

In the next stall was a trotter from Tennessee with a sore back muscle. "Doc" pressed his finger into the spot and the horse winced. Then he used acupuncture in the sensitive area. Just a few deftly placed needles and the racehorse settled down. He turned and looked at the white-haired vet with obvious gratitude.

Things like that happen all the time at Wheatley Hall Farm, McKibbin's internationally known clinic for racehorses. When all else fails, the advice given at racetracks across the continent is "take him to see Doc McKibbin."

McKibbin began using lasers and acupuncture in the mid-seventies. Since then he's treated hundreds of pacers and trotters that had been considered hopeless cases. But racing forms tell a different story. As Doc says, "to us, success shows at the wire."

A couple of his staff of five young, devoted assistants were in the process of feeding statistical evidence into a computer set up in one of the ramshackle offices. As one of them put it, "Horsemen don't come here for decor. They come for cures."

They hope the statistics will counter the criticism levelled at the clinic by some veterinarians. As far as I could gather, most are teachers of veterinary medicine at various universities.

They claim that McKibbin hasn't handled a sufficient number of cases to open up a whole new field of therapy.

At universities in the States, "Doc" is often referred to as "that crazy Canadian".

Of course, Alexander Graham Bell was known by his neighbours in Brantford as "Crazy Bell." And Edison and Henry Ford were considered a bit nuts too.

That's the way it goes it you don't run with the pack. Peculiarity breeds contempt.

Fall Fairs

The more I travel the province, and it works out to about 4,000 miles a month, the more I appreciate it. Especially at harvest time.

I like to visit Fall Fairs, the Niagara peninsula, Holland Marsh and the flatlands of Western Ontario. To the more fortunate of us, there's an aura of abundance. Closer to home, I've seen the joy in my wife's face when she brings in the first tomatoes from her garden.

The roadside stands on highways and country roads are bulging with fresh fruit and vegetables. It's a wonderful time of the year.

Of course, most of us are on the receiving end. The farmer and his family, perhaps the most underrated members of our lopsided society, have to put up with the bugs, weeds and all the other irritations that put barriers in their path.

And every once in awhile, Mother Nature gets mad at man and starts to throw things around her kitchen. Like hail, wind and flash floods. Then she pouts and won't even throw the water out of the dishpan. So we get no rain at all.

But even the economic pressures of farming these days seem to be momentarily forgotten at the Fall Fairs.

Livestock is proudly displayed. There are cattle, goats, sheep and snorting pigs. Magnificent Clydesdales, Belgians and Percherons clip-clop through the fairgrounds. Well-groomed roadsters go whirling around the tracks, their owners and trainers hanging on for dear life. Show horses and ponies prance around in front of the judges. Everybody looks very serious. After all, there's a red or blue ribbon at stake.

In the buildings, the prize pumpkin, potatoes, turnips and tomatoes form a backdrop as city and country people meet.

There's admiration for the artistry of quilts and crafts and a touch of nostalgia while gazing at the mouth-watering cakes and pies from Mom's oven.

The Fall Fair is the showcase for country living and the harvest. No one is in any great rush and you get the feeling that all's right with the world.

But human nature being what is is, there's always something to complain about. At harvest time when I stop at those fruit and vegetable stands, I get a feeling of frustration.

Everything comes at once. The plums, pears and peaches all arrive at about the same time. We just get a bit of a breather, and the apples appear. Our stomach can't take it all in, and we take the only way out. We eat what we can, and what we can't, we can.

Oldest Pilot

One nippy, windy January morning I took off in a small Cessna plane from the Brantford Flying Club with Dick Pearson at the controls.

If you're interested in flying you may have heard of him. He's Canada's oldest active pilot. He was an incredible 90 years of age when I met him.

Pearson is short, stocky and in top flight physical condition. As a pilot, he's required to have regular medical check-ups. His friend Andy Hamilton who's just a kid of 58, says the doctors make Dick's tests as tough as they can. But they never ground him. They can't. At 90, he was something of a physical phenomenon.

In the sky, his spirits soar as high as the planes he flies. As we cruised over his home town of Brantford, he said that although he's had a licence for close to half a century he still gets a thrill out of it all. "It's like being on a magic carpet," he chuckled.

We were in his friend Andy's plane. Dick sold his own plane last year because his insurance rates had gone sky high.

When we came down and went over to the clubhouse for a coffee, I noticed that the younger pilots have a great respect for the vibrant old aviator. He's admired for his knowledge, ability and experience.

"He's very steady," one pilot was telling me. "He was trained in the old school and he still walks around the plane to check everything. He goes by the check list."

Dick, a retired machinist, married for the first time when he was 74. His wife has been ill in recent years, but he visits her daily at a nursing home. He says that to stay healthy he touches his toes 100 times, and twists at the waist 200 times every morning.

They were planning a big party for Dick when I was there. All his old flying buddies were invited. The members gave me a sneak preview of the awards he was going to get, including one from The Canadian Hall of Fame.

You could tell it was going to be quite an affair. A real wing-ding. They'd be flying high. You could bank on it!

Beau and Eileen are students of the trade and hammer home the point that blacksmiths don't shoe horses.
photo by: D.L. Hunsberger

Forge and Anvil

You can learn alot about blacksmithing from Dean and Eileen Piesner. They're a couple of young blacksmiths in the village of St. Jacobs.

For example, a blacksmith doesn't shoe horses. That's the job of people called farriers.

"Blacksmiths used to make farm equipment, tools and things like that," Dean told me. "These days they make functional and decorative wrought-iron products," he said.

"When machines took over during the Industrial Revolution blacksmiths had to turn to shoeing horses to make a living and that's what caused the confusion," he added.

The couple came to St. Jacobs in the Kitchener-Waterloo district after running a blacksmith shop in Nova Scotia for some years. They had a chance to build an addition on Jon Martin's traditional shop which is right on the main street of St. Jacobs where tourism began to boom in the late 70's.

Dean and Eileen are in their 30's, are self taught and use the familiar forge and anvil. They make woodstove tools, door knockers, Christmas tree stands and weather-vanes. And they make ingenious iron puzzles that tourists gobble up for gifts.

I also learned that there's a renaissance in blacksmithing. A real revival. "The renaissance is just beginning," says Dean. "Young people are gaining a proficiency that hasn't existed in 50 years and the more work that's being done the more the craft is in demand. There's room for another 1,000 blacksmiths in Canada if there was some way they could be trained," he claims.

Once called the king of trades, blacksmithing almost disappeared beteween 1920 and 1970. Dean says if it hadn't been for the recent renaissance blacksmithing would have died out.

Dean and Eileen are representative of a new breed of blacksmith. They're students of the craft.

In their small office adjacent to the shop, are books about the history of blacksmithing and old blacksmithing techniques. They also subscribe to various trade magazines and are members of the Artist Blacksmiths Association of America.

They attend workshops called "Hammer Ins" which are held periodically in different parts of the continent.

Perhaps you remember the poem that begins "Under the spreading chestnut tree, the village smithy stands..."

These days, apparently the smithy is more likely to be standing there reading a trade paper or planning a trip to a "Hammer In" down in Southern California or someplace to find out what's new in the old business.

Central & Eastern Ontario

Boldt Castle

Recently, we took a tour boat from Gananoque down through the Thousand Islands to Boldt Castle on Heart Island. It's on the American side of the St. Lawrence. You may have heard of the castle and its romantic, but tragic history.

It was built at the turn of the century by American hotel magnate George Boldt. It was to be a present for his beloved wife, Louise. First he bought an island and transformed it into the shape of a heart. Extensive plans were drawn up, and the work began in 1900.

For more than three years, 300 workmen and 120 stonemasons using St. Lawrence granite, laboured to construct the massive fairyland-type castle. There were 100 rooms, each with a fireplace that had a mantle of imported marble. There were tapestries from Europe. No expense was spared.

Suddenly, in the summer of 1904, a telegram arrived at the island which read, "Stop all work. Mrs. Boldt is dead."

The workmen left immediately. Boldt never returned to Heart Island. Over the years, his gift of love was neglected. It began to crumble. Vandals wrote lurid graffiti on the oak-panelled walls.

There were rumours that Louise hadn't died at all. It was said that she had run off with her chauffeur. The rumours became part of the castle's legend. No one knew where Louise was buried. Boldt said nothing. By the time Boldt died, after a career that took him from hotel waiter to owner of New York's Waldorf-Astoria Hotel and a variety of other interests, the castle was a shambles.

Then a few years ago, the Thousand Islands Bridge Authority took over. They decided to restore the dilapidated towers, the mahogany bannisters on the staircases, the tunnels, the yacht houses, the arches, the broken sculpture.

A small team of restorers, headed by a dedicated young man named Dale Fikes, has already made considerable progress, although the project will take years to complete.

Fikes is something of an authority on the castle and the legends surrounding it. He was telling me that Louise Boldt died after a lengthy illness and was buried in New York's Woodlawn Cemetery. Her husband is buried beside her. So much for the mysterious rumours.

In the end, the fairytale castle became not a gift of love, but a monument to love. But it may be that other men in another era will fulfill Boldt's dream, and someday, the castle will again stand proudly amid the Thousands Islands of the River.

Birdhouse City

Brakes squeal. Heads turn. Wide-eyed little kids press their noses to car windows. They can hardly wait to get out and take a look at Birdhouse City.

They tell me that Birdhouse City is the only attraction of its kind on the continent. It's on the outskirts of the picturesque town of Picton, down near the Bay of Quinte. You can see the complex from the highway as you drive into Picton past the Macauley Mountain Conservation Area.

I'd never heard of it before, or even read anything about it. But like everyone else who sees it for the first time, I stared in surprise and admiration.

Birdhouse City consists of 92 birdhouses set up on poles over a six-acre site. The houses are built to resemble various public buildings and landmarks in Prince Edward County.

For example, you can walk around the streets of Picton and see such things as the historic courthouse, the old churches, the fire hall, and so on, then go over to Birdhouse City and see the same thing in a setting that's strictly for the birds!

The idea was dreamed up by some of the Macauley staff members. A few years ago they built a few birdhouses during the winter months. One of them was modelled on the Massasauga Hotel, a showplace in the district around 1878. Another was a nearby lighthouse.

Then they got the notion of getting the community involved. They began asking people to build additional dwelling places for the many varieties of birds that inhabit the region.

The idea caught on. Schoolchildren, youth groups, service clubs, cubs, scouts, seniors and businessmen built all sorts of model houses of landmarks for what became known as Birdhouse City.

The architectural students at the local high school went to work. Street signs were put up. It became a planned community with a general store, schools, churches, hotels — the whole works!

The residents, many of them martins, love the place. It's hard to find an apartment on Swallow Hill Road.

Of course, they're quite well-to-do. They go south in the winter and that sort of thing. There are no taxes. And to think they got all those beautiful houses for a song!

The Philoxians

Down around the village of Marlbank near Kingston, there's a farm called "Philoxia." It's not a cult or a commune. It's more like a big family, living an alternate lifestyle. But it's not the usual back-to-the-land sort of thing.

At first glance, the farm appears to be a mish-mash of boards, birds and animals. There are friendly dogs, cats, goats and donkeys and lots of rare birds. It reminds you a bit of Noah's Ark.

The Philoxians themselves are rare birds. Wonderful people. When we arrived, they were working away at various projects. Some were building an addition to their rambling building. It was interesting and attractive. It was also likely to become a building inspector's nightmare. But they're such gentle people I doubt if anyone would say a word to them. Others were busy at their innumerable artistic creations and crafts.

There are 18 in the group and they range in age from 6 months to 65. The 65-year-old is the father of one of the members. Some are single, but most are married. They have taken names that are associated with ancient philosophy. A soft-spoken young man named Awanota showed us around. He said that most of them were young former city dwellers who wanted to live close to the land and do "God's work" as he put it. But he was careful to point out that they don't embrace any formal religion.

Awanota told us that the Philoxians had been at the farm for seven years. They grew their own food which consists of grains, fruit and vegetables. They have a small dining room where you can get an excellent meal for 79 cents.

There's a wood shop where the members make everything from toys to chairs. They sell their products both at the farm and at craft shows. They also have a bakery with a huge oven that can turn out 300 loaves of bread every 90 minutes. And the group has what they call the Philoxian Farm Band which plays at various functions and gives concerts.

Everywhere you go as you wander around the farm there are people weaving or painting or teaching the children in the little classroom. Educators from Queen's, U. of T. and other prestigious universities have visited to observe their teaching methods.

The villagers of Marlbank like the Philoxians. They're proud of them. Besides, they're something of a tourist attraction. One villager told us that up to 400 people will visit the farm on a Saturday in the summer. It's hard to put a label on the Philoxians. They're just hard-working, happy people who got away from it all to live in a way that seems to suit them.

The Magnetic Hill

One of the best kept secrets around the province is the existence of Ontario's Magnetic Hill. If you happen to mention the magnetic hill phenomenon, most people will say, "Oh yes, I've heard about that. There's one down in New Brunswick, isn't there?"

There is one in Moncton, New Brunswick all right, and the last I heard the government had spent five million dollars adding to it and publicizing it. But few people have ever heard of Ontario's hill which some say is even more 'magnetic' than the one in New Brunswick.

If you're unfamiliar with magnetic hills in general, they're unusual slopes where you get the sensation you're going up when you're actually going down!

Ontario's magnetic hill is in the Ottawa Valley on the outskirts of the village of Dacre, near Renfrew. I heard about it a few years ago from Bernie Bedore. He's an Ottawa Valley woodsman, writer, storyteller and creator of Joe Mufferaw, the mythical gentle giant who once inhabited the Ottawa Valley. Bernie lives near Arnprior and one day he took me over to Dacre to see the Magnetic Hill.

I would have never found it on my own. There's a tiny government sign on the main highway pointing toward the hill, but unless you were really looking you'd drive right by it.

The hill isn't very steep and it's only about 300 yards long. But when you drive over its crest, strange things begin to happen. If you stop your car halfway down and put it into neutral gear, you seem to be moving up the hill again. Backwards, as if you're being pulled back by some magnetic force. And from the outside it also appears that the car is moving back up the hill!

Not everyone gets the sensation, but many people do. I did and I was astounded!

Bernie chuckled at my amazement and explained that it was because of "the lay of the land," as he put it. There's also a stream that runs beside the hill and you'd swear it was running uphill!

I asked Bernie why the hill hadn't been publicized more. He just shook his head. "It's a more effective hill than the one in New Brunswick," he said. "But nobody knows about it and nobody takes the trouble to tell them."

It's all an optical illusion of course. But when you're sitting in your car, going uphill backwards, and apparently defying all the laws of gravity, it's quite an experience. Interesting and a bit weird.

Windmill Man

People come from many parts of the world to visit the village of Wellington, down near Trenton in Eastern Ontario. It's not so much the village itself that attracts them. It's Wellington's windmill man — Jerry Ball.

A middle-aged casual sort of guy, Jerry works out of his rambling, cluttered machine shop on the outskirts of town.

He works alone and he works seven days a week making windmills. Or if you want to be technical, windpowered generators.

He sells them for anywhere from $2,000 to $20,000. He says he's not making a fortune, but enjoys the work. One of his best markets is around Yellowknife where hydro is expensive, although he has customers in various parts of the world.

As you approach Jerry's place, you see three windmills reaching up into the sky. They heat and provide electricity to his home and workshop for under $200 a year.

The windmills are connected to a backup of batteries. When more power is being produced than can be used at the moment, the excess is stored in battery tanks and used when there's no wind. Jerry checks his wind speed indicator several times a day. Usually it reads about 15 mph.

Ball is a former tool and die maker. He's also an inventor who has patented several items. So if he can't find things he needs to make the windmills, or can't afford them, he simply makes them.

Ironically, right next door to Ball's set-up is an Ontario Hydro installation. Everybody who visits gets quite a kick out of it.

But Jerry and Hydro are good neighbours. When they've got the energy they swap a few kilowatts over the back fence!

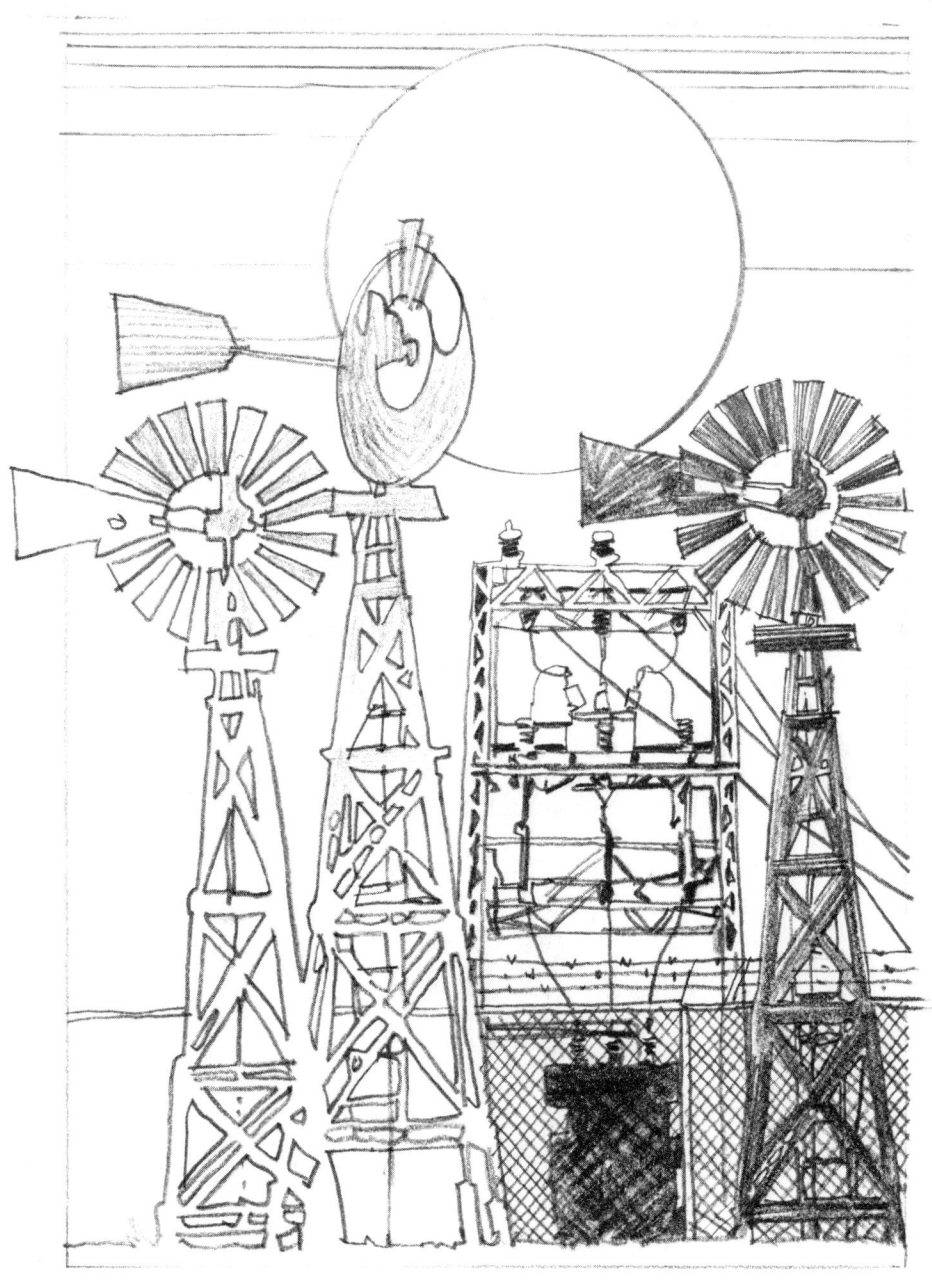

Fence Viewers

Whether you know it or not, there are likely at least three fence viewers in your community.

Under Ontario law, property owners have always shared the responsibility for fences between their properties. In the past, when disputes arose about matters involving a fence, an arbitrator was called in to try to settle the problem. The arbitrator was called a fence viewer.

They've been around since 1826. They're appointed by municipalities and they still exist. I met two of them in the Town of Vaughan, a few miles north of Toronto.

John Becker and Glen Norcliffe were telling me that they get $25 a call. But they don't get too many calls. John says he's only had two calls since he took the job a few years ago. So he augments his income by being Vice-President of York University. Apparently Glen hasn't had any calls at all so far. He says he found things so tough that he was forced to support his wife and children by being a professor of Geography at York.

Both feel they are well qualified for their jobs as fence viewers. But it seems there just isn't that much work for fence viewing anymore. They're both brutally blunt. They openly admit they're both moonlighting!

When we all stopped chuckling about their miserable plight, I learned that these days most fence disputes are settled over a cup of coffee. And in most areas, fence viewers are appointed from among public works employees who are not paid extra for the work.

There's not much glamour in the job. It hasn't the devil-may-care flair of dog-catcher, for example. But it's nice to know that when we're faced with a fence dispute there's someone out there who cares. Someone who can be impartial. Someone who is on the fence and can provide defenses for our fences.

The Painting Priest

I watched Father Ted Koufas painting murals on the dome of the Ukrainian Catholic Church in Welland. He'd been working on them for months.

As I looked at the beautiful paintings I noticed that he had 14 apostles in a big mural of The Last Supper. That's two more than the usual number. When I asked him why, he had a simple explanation:

"I had enough space on the wall so I threw in a couple of extra apostles."

That's the kind of guy he is. He doesn't go by the book. And where apostles are concerned he sure doesn't paint by numbers.

He paints what are called icons. That's a Byzantine type of mural first done around the fourth century when they didn't worry about time and space the way we do.

Father Ted has an indefinite leave of absence from his parish in Toronto and goes from church to church painting icons. He has a long waiting list of churches where, as he puts it, the walls and ceilings are "just crying out to be painted."

The Painting Priest traces his interest in this type of religious painting to his childhood when he saw huge icons in the church his family attended. Later, while studying for the priesthood, he also studied iconography. Now he climbs scaffolds and reaches up with his brush in the manner of Michelangelo.

Incidentally, Father Ted has a twin brother in New York, Father Philip Koufas, who is also a painting priest and is doing the same thing — painting icons in various churches.

The brothers are among only eight artists doing this type of painting on the North American continent.

Cactus Grower

Did you know that the largest grower of cactus on North America is a 70-year old dynamo who lives in Dundas?

Dundas, by the way, is a small town near Hamilton. The grower is Ben Veldhuis who has acres of greenhouses on the edge of town that are packed with cactus.

Ben and his family sell over three million cacti a year in 1,200 varieties. They ship them across continents from Vancouver to Hong Kong, from Barbados to Europe.

They have cactus plants with names that would throw even a Latin teacher into a tizzy. Some are 25-feet high. Others are those squat, dome-like types that you see in landscape gardens. Then there are thousands and thousands of little plants peeking out at you from their greenhouse beds.

Ben spends about five months of the year travelling the world buying and selling seeds. He's been doing it for years. He's big, bluff with a booming voice and usually has a black cigar stuck in his mouth. He's a busy man and a knowledgeable one. So is his wife, and his son, and his brother, and his sister. They're all into the act and none of them seem to slow down.

Trucks are coming and going. People are on the phone taking orders. Groups of seniors and schoolchildren are being shown around.

I stood in the middle of it all while Ben and his sister Martha told me about the care of the water-thrifty prickly plants.

But the cactus plants are in no rush. It may take some of them three months just to germinate and a century to become sizeable plants.

Rendezvous for Seniors

One day I decided to get away from it all. I'd get away from travelling the highways and biways and bushy-tailed young cameramen. I'd take the day off and be with my own kind.

So I went to Toronto's Harbourfront for what's called the "Rendezvous for Seniors." It's not publicized much, but it's likely the biggest ongoing activity for seniors in the country.

Harbourfront is a large recreational complex down near the CN Tower. It's a place where you can roam around and watch glassblowers and other craftsmen at work, or sit on the quiet patios and gaze at the sailboats out on the lake.

I visualized a nice quiet day. I expected to see seniors sitting around talking about the good old days, a few people knitting or sewing and the odd game of euchre or something.

But as I walked across the parking lot, toward the entrance of the rambling building, I heard a rumbling sound and the beat of drums in the background. Like jungle drums.

When I went in, the rumbling sound became louder. And then I saw them! Hundreds of seniors milling around! They were everywhere! And there was music and dancing and singing!

My visions of a nice quiet day were shattered. Even before I could grab a cup of coffee, I was hustled off to a class in ballroom dancing. Mind you, it was still only about 11 o'clock in the morning.

Although I'm no Fred Astaire, I managed to muddle through a couple of routines and then tried to slink off to the patio.

But it was not to be. A vibrant white-haired man led me over to a singalong, then to another hall overlooking the lake where old-time entertainers were whooping it up. They were followed by a Dixieland band playing "Sweet Georgia Brown" for a Charleston contest, with some seniors dressed as flappers of the Twenties.

I bowed out of a boat trip and an investment seminar by saying I wanted to stay and watch the Charleston contest.

Nobody seemed interested in pausing for lunch. It was early afternoon and things were just warming up.

I got out of there. I was feeling the strain. As I was leaving someone was saying about 20,000 seniors attend the Rendezvous activities every year.

While walking back to the car, very slowly, I began to wonder how all those seniors manage to handle the pressures of retirement.

The Rockhounds

People from all over the world have scrambled up and down in the rocky hills that surround the village of Bancroft in Northeastern Ontario.

They're called "rockhounds." Collectors of minerals. And Bancroft draws them like a magnet. It's estimated there are about 500 different kinds of minerals in the area.

One day we joined some rockhounds at the Princess Mine to look for sodalite. It's a blue, semi-precious gem. The Princess is on the outskirts of the village and is loaded with sodalite. It was opened in 1890 when mining was booming in Bancroft. It's changed hands several times and currently is operated by Paul Rasmussen.

Paul is a big, burly Dutchman who like other mining men around Bancroft will talk your head off as soon as you mention minerals. He'll give you the history of Bancroft's mines — most of which no longer exist. He'll give a novice a concise explanation of the mysteries of minerology. He never runs out of steam.

Paul's mine is mostly a one-man operation. With a fat cigar sticking out of his mouth, he sinks his hand drill into the rock and big chunks fall off. The drill shakes the bejeepers out of him but he doesn't seem to notice. He shouts above the noise of the drill, telling you where to look for the good stuff.

We'd been given a mallet and a pail. After persistent pounding I managed to knock out a small piece of rock. It had a lot of dark blue sodalite in it.

Later, we made our way back to Paul's workshop where he turns out rings, pendants and so on.

He put my small rock under a wheel called a diamond saw. He whittled it down to a flat bit of blue sodalite, marked it out for a design and polished it. Presto! I had a gem I had mined myself.

When we went back to the Sword Motel, where we stay up there, owner Ken Willcocks was saying that Paul plans to fly rockhounds over from Europe on a weekly basis, to visit sites around Bancroft.

It might take awhile to get the project off the ground, but Rasmussen's the man to do it.

Spend a morning with Paul and you're hooked! You've become a rockhound.

Joey the Beaver

The beaver is a little animal that follows his instincts come hell or high water. He stubbornly persists in doing what beavers do for a living. And he gets into a lot of trouble that way.

Farmers, especially in Southern Ontario, are always complaining about the beaver. So are the people who take care of the highways. But they invariably smile a bit when they beef about "those darn beavers." The same sort of smile we have for a kid who raids the cookie jar.

The beaver's whole problem is building dams in the wrong places. That is, as far as man is concerned. Of course, from the beaver's point of view it's the other way around. If man begins busting beaver dams, the beaver likely curses away at him because he's monkeying around with the beaver's work.

These things were running through my mind recently as I was getting a TV news item together about the damage beavers have done in Simcoe County. Beaver dams have flooded a number of farmers' fields and at one point on Highway 11, just north of Barrie a beaver dam almost caused a small flood on the highway one year.

Along the line, I renewed my acquaintance with Joey. Richard Toth of the Ministry of Natural Resources arranged it. Joey is one of the few tame beavers in the province. He was an orphan until rescued in infancy and turned over to Lloyd and Helen Cook of Barrie. They're highly qualified and were given a special licence to keep the little beaver as a pet.

Joey is what you might call a public relations beaver. He's now an adult and for some time has been travelling the classroom circuit and the wildlife shows. Consequently he's a very busy beaver.

We wanted to show a beaver building a dam. Ordinarily, beavers work at night and we wouldn't have much of a chance. But guided by Lloyd and Helen, our pal Joey swam a stream with a branch in his mouth and we got some good pictures. Then we cut to a nearby dam. It had a lodge where the beaver stores food.

So thanks to Joey we were able to show something about the lifestyle of the beaver and some of the problems that result.

I learned a lot about the beaver that day and how he fits into the balance of nature. Of course, we Canadians think so much of the industrious rodent that his picture is on our five-cent coins.

But there's another side to the coin. Although the beaver is undoubtedly a valuable asset, at times he can be a dam nuisance.

Holland Marsh

Most of us take Holland Marsh for granted. We know it's Ontario's largest and most famous vegetable garden and people who regularly go up Highway 400 to cottage country have likely glanced at it with casual interest hundreds of times.

They may have some vague notion that the vast farmland was named after the Dutch farmers who first settled in the district. And that's about all most of us know about it.

But as in so many cases with familiar landmarks, there's a lot more than meets the eye. The Marsh is far larger than the part of it that can be seen from the highway. It's about 16 miles long. Nor was it named after the Dutch farmers. It got its name from Major A. Holland who surveyed the area in 1830 at the request of Lord Simcoe.

I learned these tidbits when I dropped around to what's called the Muck Research Station, just beside the highway, to meet Matt Valk. Matt is Director of the station and has been studying the Marsh for about 40 years. Ever since he came from Holland.

He can give you some surprising information. For example, there are really six marshes extending west from Lake Simcoe. The Holland is just one of them. In a good year, farmers harvest 120,000 tons of carrots alone!

The organic soil, consisting of muck, peat and silt, has a depth varying from a few inches to 90 feet in some places!

In the early days, no one had much success farming the marshes. Then in the early thirties, 18 families of knowledgeable, hard-working Dutch immigrants arrived. They knew about dikes and drainage and before long, were bringing in phenomenal crops.

They also founded a village called Ansnorveldt. Some of their descendants are still there. The village is about five miles east of Highway 400, tucked away on the edge of the Marsh.

I've always thought of Ansnorveldt as a little bit of Holland. It's likely because of my reaction when I first saw it about five years ago.

It was a beautiful spring morning. The little village with its tidy houses was spotless. There were tulips everywhere. And I noticed a fair-haired older man walking out to his mailbox on the roadside. He was wearing wooden shoes.

Esmond's Tea Room

Esmond's Tea Room is a colourful little place set among the pines at Lake St. Peter in Northeastern Ontario.

In order to get there you have to go through Bancroft, then a few hamlets with names like Bird's Creek and Maynooth, until finally you hit the country road that leads to Esmond's.

Any marketing analyst would tell you that trying to operate a business in that location would be sheer madness. Any accountant would just shudder at the suggestion.

But Esmond's Tea Room has a regular and faithful clientele. It does an excellent business day and night. And it's mostly because of Esmond himself. He's even more colourful than the brightly painted tea room!

Although it was bitterly cold the day we arrived, Esmond greeted us in a summer shirt and shorts. He appeared to be about 50. Tall, lithe and built like an Olympic swimmer, he positively bristled with vibrant health. Yet Esmond Skidmore was crowding seventy at that time!

He eats and serves good food. He does his own baking. Uses no

Esmond and Bill get together to entertain at Esmond's Tea Room where the host provides tea and positive philosophy for his guests.
photo by: Robert Lyons

additives and nothing but stoneground flour.

He bathes daily in the nearby lake. When it's frozen over, he has a snow bath. He did it while we were there late in February. Bundled up in my parka, I watched in amazement as he gleefully wallowed around in the snow, wearing nothing but swimming trunks.

Bancroft writer and bookseller, Bob Lyons, who told us about the tea room, says Esmond's tea is the best he's ever tasted. Bob, who's travelled the world and has had mint tea in Morocco, Indian tea and London blends, still swears by Esmond's brew.

Esmond has a one-man operation. He's cook, waiter and entertainer. He play requests on a piano set over in a corner of the room. As a positive thinker, he also listens to problems and gives advice to some of the patrons. Tea and sympathy. I asked him how the tea room managed to survive in the early years.

"I couldn't lose," he laughed. "I was broke when I got here. I've been a drop-out for 30 years, but I love life. Maybe people come here to see if some of it will rub off."

Monastery Row

One beautiful winter morning, I went back to Hockley Valley, that idyllic area of the countryside on the outskirts of Orangeville.

The pines and spruce clustered in the rolling hills were heavily laden with snow that had fallen the night before. Sunbeams were bouncing around and the valley glistened.

Farmers, artists, writers and just plain folks live in the valley. And in recent years, its tranquillity has attracted religious orders.

There are now four of them that I know of, all located within a stone's throw of each other. They're neighbours. And I've always thought of the string of them as Monastery Row.

The first to arrive were the Franciscan Friars. They're a teaching order. Some of them look like Robin Hood's Friar Tuck. And Friar Terry, who showed me around, was just as jolly. None of them seemed to mind the exuberant inner city kids who were there for a week of nature study.

A few hundred yards from the rambling monastery, the teaching sisters of the order, the Felecians, live in a picturesque farmhouse.

About a mile down the road are the Christian Brothers. You can get a glimpse of the squat cottages they occupy as you travel along Highway 9.

The Brothers are an Irish order and the Monastery is a training school for novices.

The newest arrivals to Monastery Row are the Cistercian Monks, formerly known as Trappist. They have a large modern building and one of the most beautiful chapels I've seen in years.

The monks were praying silently when I went into the chapel. Lay people also had their heads bowed in prayer. They were there on a retreat from the hurly-burly of city life.

In the spring, the monks will farm their 300 acres and eventually will become self-sufficient.

Father Justin, the abbot, was saying that they had yet to meet the members of the other religious communities in the valley.

So although their order is more than 1,500 years old, the Cistercians are still the new kids on the block on Monastery Row.

Ice Fishing

Every year I try to get out for a day of ice fishing. Sometimes I go out on Penetang Bay, a few miles from our farm.

When I feel particularly energetic, I might take a run up to North Bay and plod over the ice to one of the huts on Lake Nipissing.

But when I'm in an expansive mood, I drive over to Beaverton to one of the fish hut camps and go out on Lake Simcoe by taxi!

The place I find most convenient is Floyd Hales Huts, although there are about 30 other operators on the big lake.

The taxis are not of the usual variety. They're more like a small bus with skis and tracks. They skim across the ice to the huts which are about two miles out on the lake.

I remember one blustery winter day when Floyd was taking us out, we hit a series of white-outs. That didn't bother Floyd a bit. He knew exactly where he was going. His secret was simple. Fish hut operators blaze a trail with small pine trees they plant in the ice when the season opens. On stormy days they just follow the pines to shore.

When Floyd retired, Bill and Gale Vieveen bought the business. Bill worked for Floyd for a number of years and has been fishing the lake since he was a boy. Bill is quite an authority. He knows the spots the perch and the herring frequent and where the whitefish and lake trout roam.

The last time I went ice fishing with him, Bill drove us out to meet a group of fishermen from Michigan. Global's veteran cameraman, Terry Culbert, was with us. Terry has shot film in various parts of the world and has had all sorts of adventures, but had never been ice fishing!

As we left in the taxi, he seemed a bit skeptical about the whole thing. But when we arrived at the site and went into one of the roomy huts where some of the Americans were fishing, his eyes lit up.

The seats of foam and leather, the propane furnace in the corner, the coziness of the hut and the fishermen looking over their catch of about 30 lake trout, were impressive. The group had lived there for three days.

"This isn't what I expected," said Terry. "I couldn't see the point of sitting in the cold waiting for fish to bite. But this is sheer luxury."

I suppose he had a point. On the other hand, most huts I've been in provide lots of protection. They look cold and barren from the outside, but inside you get a feeling of solid comfort and splendid isolation.

Pirate Ship

When I was a kid, I wanted to be a zoo-keeper. Later I changed my mind and decided to be a fireman. Still later, I switched to becoming a pirate. That was the strongest urge of all. But it too, passed away.

Then a couple of years ago I met Captain David May and got that old feeling.

Because Captain May is a pirate! And he's got a pirate ship to prove it! It's an 82-foot, 60-ton replica of "The Rattlesnake," a privateer captured by the British in 1781.

Early in the 80's, David and his wife Barbara, along with their son Stephen, began building the ship near a marina in Orillia. They got some beautiful pine from an abandoned lumber yard.

Later, they hauled it over to Jackson's Point and I went over to take another look at it. When completed, the ship will take people for short cruises on Lake Simcoe. Meanwhile, the pirate and his crew are living and working on the "Rattlesnake" hoping to launch it any time now.

"If anybody asked me to build something like this, it would cost at least a million dollars," says David. "Doing a lot of our own labour, we've been able to cut corners."

Plans for the future include sailing the ship to Chicago and eventually a voyage from England to Australia.

Captain May's wife says that when David first mentioned the idea about ten years ago she took it with a grain of salt.

"Like most wives, I went along with it thinking it was a crazy scheme he'd soon forget," says Barbara. "Then I realized he meant it. My first thought was that at least I was going to have a modern bathroom."

And a modern bathroom the ship consignment will have. Along with a well-equipped galley, two diesel engines and a full consignment of black powder cannon!

These modern buccaneers may even fly the Jolly Roger at times. Maybe even sail the Spanish Main.

It's the stuff that dreams are made of.

Dream Come True

When I was a kid I used to dream of being a fireman when I grew up. I guess a lot of us did in those days.

Well, my boyhood dreams came true. And far beyond my wildest expectations. I was Honorary Fire Chief for a day in the Southwestern Ontario town of Simcoe.

The occasion was the town's annual Friendship Festival. Part of the celebration was "Muster '83," the Simcoe Firefighter's antique apparatus show. It was an international event with old pumpers from New York, Michigan and Pennsylvania on display, along with trucks from various parts of Ontario.

There was a big parade to open the whole thing. I was in the Fire Chief's car wearing a chief's cap with gold braid. I didn't drive the car. Dave Harriot, the Deputy Chief, did that, leaving me free to wave to the applauding crowds.

What I didn't know was that the applause was for the beautiful 19-year-old Festival Queen who was riding right behind us on a decorated float. I finally caught on, but kept waving anyway. Just in case.

But later on, I had my moment of glory. The mayor presented me with a big white chief's hat, and an impressive plaque commemorating the event.

There were about 200 firefighters and their wives and children attending the festival. After the parade, the judging of the antique equipment got underway. The old pumpers had been carefully restored by the various brigades. There was an old horse-drawn vehicle from 1917. And Simcoe's own 1936 Bickle won another award. That vehicle has won about 20 awards at shows in both Canada and the United States.

After that there were demonstrations of speed and skill in firefighting. Simcoe's traditional rival is the volunteer brigade from Gasport, a little town in Michigan. Simcoe won some events, but lost in the water barrel competition.

Then the wives took over. Wearing their husband's outfits, they put on a dazzling display of skill.

But the real stars were the children. In their outsized equipment they stole the show as they handled the heavy hose with surprising finesse. To top it off, the Simcoe kids beat Gasport.

I stood there in my big white Fire Chief's hat, eating a hot dog. It was a day to remember.

Raising Crickets

Visualize yourself taking care of two and a half million crickets for a living. That's what Mel Rowe and Rose Gale do.

The couple keep the small creatures in tanks on the third floor of an abandoned warehouse in Brantford and are believed to be Canada's only cricket breeders.

They sell them to zoos and suppliers of pet shops as food for fish and reptiles, and they ship about 40,000 a week.

They're not ordinary crickets. They're from California, and you can hardly hear them! One reason is that many are about the size of a pinhead. Another is that they have much softer bodies than the black crickets we're used to, and make less noise when they rub their legs against their wings, which is apparently a mating call.

Mel and Rose started the business some years ago with 80 imported crickets.

"We made a lot of mistakes," says Mel. "Nobody knew anything about crickets. Even the library had nothing, so we had to experiment. It was trial and error all the way."

One of the biggest challenges they faced was finding food for their livestock. They finally developed a food that's a mixture of grain, but they keep the formula a secret. Temperature is another big factor. If there's a draft, or too much humidity, the crickets will die as soon as they're hatched.

There are close to 100 tanks swarming with crickets in various stages of development. They are packed in cases and sent in a special truck to their various destinations. The Metro Toronto Zoo alone takes 5,000 a week.

With two and a half million crickets in the background you'd expect an ungodly racket, and if you were dealing with our rugged black Canadian crickets there likely would be. But you can hardly hear these little critters. There's just a soft, soothing murmur, very pleasing to the ear.

Mildred M. Mahoney poses beside one of the doll's houses she has restored. Her collection is thought to be the world's largest.

The Dollhouse Gallery

I used to think of Fort Erie in terms of the Peace Bridge, Crystal Beach, and the Race Track. Now, I'm more inclined to think of it as the home of the "Mildred M. Mahoney Silver Jubilee Doll's House Gallery."

Mildred, a petite 65-year-old widow, has been buying up dollhouses from various parts of the world for 30 years. At last count, she had 145 of them. But it's no small-time operation. Her miniature real estate is valued at $1.5 million — likely the biggest collection of its kind in the world.

Most of the houses have been restored and are displayed at Bertie Hall — which is a story in itself. A Fort Erie landmark, located a couple of miles north of the Peace Bridge, it was built in 1826. King Edward VII stayed there upon occasion, and the red brick mansion's basement is said to have been used to smuggle slaves to freedom, and later, during Prohibition, to smuggle booze into Canada.

Mrs. Mahoney's collection fills almost every room of the big house. Her most prized possession is a $40,000 five storey English manor built in 1810. Another favourite is called the Mystery House, because nobody knows too much about its origin except that it was made in the U.S. in 1880. It's filled with turn-of-the-century furniture made from cigar boxes by tramps — knights of the open road — who sold them for a meal or a night's lodging.

Ivy climbs the walls of some dollhouses. Others have little sewing rooms with tiny spools of thread and sewing machines. A kitchen will have food on the table and oil paintings grace the walls.

Over a thousand tourists a month visit the Gallery, many on bus tours from various parts of Canada and the United States.

"It's a nostalgic trip for a lot of people," says Mildred. "Older people seem to get the most pleasure out of the houses, and seeing the artifacts of the past."

She doesn't merely collect the houses, she also does the restoration of them in a workshop at her home a few miles away.

Apparently you can commission someone to make you a dollhouse, but the hobby is so popular that you'll likely have to face a waiting list of up to two years. The prices of the custom miniatures range from $200 to $25,000.

Those little houses are big business these days.

Mr. Kite

One summer day I relived my boyhood days. I flew a kite. The old exhilaration of getting it up in the air and watching it soar into the wild blue yonder came back once again.

I tugged on the twine, wondering if my kite would stay high in the sky, or whether the fickle breezes would disappear and my kite would plummet into the tree tops.

Beside me was Ken Lewis. With the grace of an old pro, he was flying a huge kite he had made himself. It was about 20 feet square. A monstrous kite of many colours. Ken has made thousands of kites and has flown them in many countries. But not just for the fun of it. He's thought to be the only man in the world who makes his living flying kites!

Known professionally as "Mr. Kite-Canada," he puts on displays at Ontario Place in the summer, and various parks in Florida during the winter. He's written books and articles about kites. He's an authority.

Now 73, he looks about 60 and has a showman's flair and finesse.

He works out of Mississauga. He has a rented shack in a farmer's field — probably the only field left in the middle of Mississauga. But he doesn't call his shack a shack.

"Join me over in my studio," he says with a dramatic wave of the hand. The studio which Ken refers to occasionally as a "laboratory," is packed with kites. His workbench is in a corner. The kites are folded, but as he hauls them out and spreads them on the ground, the variety is astounding.

There are heavy-duty kites for high winds, and gossamer-light ones for use when there is almost no breeze at all. There are crates, diamonds, butterflies, bees, and even one shaped like a giant pickle which Lewis made for a canning company.

Although the world record for kite-flying is roughly seven miles, Lewis says amateurs should stay below 350 feet to avoid trouble with aviation regulations.

At Ontario Place, where he might have six or seven kites in the air at one time, he prefers not to go above 100 feet.

Ken says there's a great therapeutic value in flying kites. People in pressure jobs find the hobby helpful. So if the tensions of a topsy-turvy world are getting you down — go fly a kite!

Ginseng Farm

For some time motorists going north on Highway 400 wondered about a low wooden structure being built beside the highway.

It's about 15 miles north of Toronto and when they started putting it up, people thought it might be an experimental vineyard or something like that. There were thousands of posts set about six feet apart. But then a roof of slats was put over the whole thing, and motorists didn't know what to think.

I finally got around to finding out about it. If you're from Asia you probably knew all along. It's a ginseng farm.

To those who live in the Orient, ginseng is a general tonic, a cure-all. It's a plant that's used to make tea, soups, just about anything. You can even smoke it.

The farm is owned by Sung Sa Lee and his family, who came over from Korea ten years ago. The Lees already have a ginseng farm over on the other side of the highway toward Aurora. They have about 35 acres in all. They aren't the only ginseng farmers in the province. There are some down in the Waterford area near Lake Erie.

Lee's daughter Connie is the only one of the seven people who work the farms who speaks fluent English. And she knows plenty about ginseng.

It takes five years for a crop to mature. And Lee's first crop was harvested in 1983. The entire crop was snapped up by buyers in Hong Kong.

Connie showed me around both farms. She was telling me that the wooden slats on top of the posts are protection from the sun, not the cold.

Our winters are no problem since ginseng grows in northern parts of Asiatic countries that have climates similar to our own.

In the Far East, apparently, ginseng is looked upon as a real boon to mankind — good for aches and pains, nausea, flu and that tired run-down feeling.

I suppose you might call it the Geritol of the Orient.

The 19th Century Man

Some years ago, Toronto businessman John Clark decided he didn't like the direction our modern technological society was taking. He decided to go back in time and be an early 19th century man. To all appearances he did.

He left the city and moved to the Tottenham area, east of Orangeville, where he opened a workshop and began to make muzzle loaders for a living. They're those big bulky guns the early settlers used, and very popular with collectors these days. He knew something about making the guns — it had been a hobby.

But he went further than that. He changed his whole lifestyle. He threw out his three-piece Bay Street suits, and dressed in 19th century clothing. At first, the villagers in Tottenham regarded him as some sort of weirdo, and his friends thought he'd taken leave of his senses, but that didn't bother him a bit. He changed his thinking too, and his attitudes. And somehow he contrived to live in today's world without really being a part of it. On the surface, anyway.

Clark says he's not alone. The trend toward more natural living by many people is because, like himself, they've become dissatisfied with what he calls our superficial, artificial 20th century way of life.

I enjoy watching John at work. He's a true craftsman — a stickler for authenticity and detail. It takes him a minimum of 100 hours to make one of his antique guns. The muzzle loaders are not only fine examples of workmanship, most of them are accurate up to 100 yards.

To walk into his workshop is to walk into another century. You're surrounded by powder horns, leather hunting bags and beads — the trappings of another era.

In one respect however, John Clark is quite modern. His custom-made muzzle loaders can cost anywhere from $600 to $3,000. And a spin off from being a 19th century gunsmith is his work in movies and TV — he's often called upon to play parts in films calling for pioneer types.

But on the whole, Clark seems to have combined the best of two worlds. He likes his work, his century-old way of life and by modern standards is "doing well" as the saying goes. He's always trying to keep up with all the orders he has. In fact, for Gunsmith Clark, business is really booming!

Last Duel Park

In the town of Perth in the Ottawa Valley, there's a little park on the banks of the Tay River which runs through the town. It's called "Last Duel Park," and it's where the last duel ever fought in Canada took place.

Close to the river is a gravestone marking the spot where Robert Lyon, a law student, was killed on a murky morning in June, back in 1833.

Some years ago a Little Theatre group re-enacted the event for us and every time I visit the area, I recall the story.

It all started with a beautiful girl named Elizabeth Hughes. It seems that Robert Lyon made a disparaging remark about her to his fellow student John Wilson who loved the lady from afar — as they used to say in the nineteenth century.

This led to fisticuffs, and later, Wilson, at the urging of friends, somewhat reluctantly, challenged Lyon to a duel with pistols. Reluctantly, because Lyon was known to be a crack shot!

The duel took place early in the morning. In the first exchange both men missed and were prepared to call it quits. But Lyon's second, another student named Le Leivre, insisted they do it over again. Le Leivre was the villain of the piece. It was later learned that he too was attracted to the beauteous Elizabeth Hughes. On the second exchange, Wilson's shot hit and killed Lyon.

By 1833 duelling was frowned upon in Ontario and Wilson was brought to trial. But in a series of legal hijinks, and apparently the sympathy of the judge and jury, he was acquitted.

And what happened to Wilson? Well, in later years, he not only married Elizabeth Hughes, despite her parents' objections, he also became a Justice of the Supreme Court!

The Herb Homestead

Tucked away in a valley in the Aurora district just north of Toronto, is the village of Kettleby. It's one of those historic, beautiful, picture-postcard places that are scattered around the province.

I went there to visit Barry Dimock at what he calls "The Herb Homestead."

It's a century-old white frame building with a small greenhouse attached where Dimock grows hundreds of herbs and plants. He's a plant consultant specializing in herbs.

But he's quick to point out that he's not involved in curing bodily ills with herbs, nor does he run a restaurant.

"I'm interested in herbs and plants in a creative way," says Dimock. "I write about them, give lectures and cooking lessons."

And for the novice gardener, Barry has plenty of surprises. I always thought geraniums smelled like geraniums and that was it. Then I watched him rub the leaves of various geranium plants. One by one he handed them to me, saying "smell them."

S'help me, he's got geraniums that smell like peppermint, orange, lemon, lime, and even roses!

He can also whip up salads using herbs and plants that will tempt even the most jaded appetites. And while he's at it, he gives you a running commentary on the history of herbs and the legends that have grown up around them.

A visit with Dimock is an educational experience. And "The Herb Homestead" is an interesting place that seems to fit right into the village of Kettleby with its Old World charm.

Clock Auction

Did you ever hear of a clock auction where there were no clocks for sale?

Sounds ridiculous, but in Mississauga there's a huge warehouse where a big flower auction takes place four mornings a week. It's called the Toronto Clock Auction and growers from various parts of Ontario gather there to buy and sell hundreds of thousands of plants and flowers.

Among the growers the auction is known simply as "The Clock". That's because of the great big clock set up in the front of a large room where the auction is held. Facing the clock are tiered rows of desks with buzzers on them.

The clock runs backwards from 100 to 1. Various lots of flowers or plants are paraded out, and the bidding begins. The hand of the clock begins to move. When the price is right the buyer presses the buzzer — maybe several buyers do. It requires concentration and lightning speed. The face of the clock registers the buyer's number. He may beat out another buyer by a fraction of a second.

The auction is operated by the Ontario Flower Growers Co-op. There are about 160 members and each is required to offer at least one lot for sale every week. Consequently the supply is plentiful.

The flowers are transported during the night, with the deadline for arrival 5 a.m. That gives the buyers a chance to look them over before the auction.

The volume boggles the mind! For example, Proben Hansen, who runs Oak Farms in Leamington, has a fleet of refrigerated trucks. He'll bring in 20,000 roses a night!

The buyers include retail florists, growers, wholesalers and agents. As they walk through the warehouse they scribble down their preferences on slips of paper. When auction time approaches they move quickly into the auction area to take their places at the desks. They buy about $7 million worth of flowers and plants a year at the auction.

By the way, you have to get up pretty early in the morning to see the buyers in action. The auction starts at 6:30 a.m. By eight o'clock it's over, and business is all wound up for another day at "The Clock".

The Buggy Man

You know it's spring when the robins return, the buds peek out from the branches of trees, and Bill Malcolmson hitches up one of his show horses and goes for a buggy ride!

Bill is a retired Barrie insurance man whose hobby is horses. He's been around horses since he was a kid and over the years has built up a showplace called Cedar Rail Farm, at Crown Hill, a few miles north of Barrie.

Currently he has eight magnificent standardbreds. They're kept in a big black barn with white trim. Just behind it is another barn — what Malcolmson calls a "buggy barn". It houses one of the most varied collection of old buggies and cutters you've ever seen. There are — and get this — 62 of them! Some date back to the 1880's.

At times, the carriages could be pretty fancy. Malcolmson's prize carriage is a Brougham built at the turn of the century. It has style, a look of quality. And Bill used it to get his daughter to the church on time when she was married.

He also has a buggy which used to be a taxi that ran between the trains and hotels in Penetanguishene. Then there's a ladies' Phaeton built in Brantford in 1888. The list goes on and on.

Down on the lower floor of the Malcolmson's century-old home is Bill's workshop. It's where he has painstakingly restored the whole collection. The hours he's put in doing it must have run into the thousands!

His den is down there too. It's a horsey room. It fairly bulges with trophies, ribbons, pictures of horses, sculptured horses, books about horses.

Malcolmson still goes to the office almost daily, but takes time out for visits by schoolchildren — and seniors. He says the kids like the buggies, but it's the seniors who really appreciate them.

As I left, there was a busload of seniors arriving. When they saw some of the buggies out on the track beside the barn, there were smiles, chuckles and squeals of delight!

Bill Malcolmson (centre) showing visitors a few of the buggies in his huge collection.

School Patrollers

Early one summer I watched a couple of school patrollers evacuate 40 youngsters from a school bus in 22 seconds.

It could have been a life and death situation. But it wasn't. It was just part of the training the patrollers get at Camp Samac in Oshawa.

The Camp itself is a surprising place. It's a beautiful Boy Scout Camp with a man-made lake. But it's tucked away about a hundred yards or so from the city's busy Simcoe Street. Unless you were looking for it, you'd miss it completely.

For the past 14 years the Ontario Motor League has rented part of the camp for a week to train school patrollers in the responsibilities of their jobs.

Pat Curran of the OML who has been coordinator of the project since it started was telling me they had about 80 kids when they started. Now there are close to 250 of them every year.

Twenty-four police officers from various parts of the province were on hand to teach the students such things as how to handle pedestrian traffic at different types of intersections, and how to assist school bus drivers. The patrollers even learn how to steer and stop the buses in case of emergency.

The day I was there, police were giving lectures and supervising drills all morning, while St. John Ambulance people gave demonstrations in elementary first aid.

The patrollers range in age from 10 to 14. I talked to Noel Johnston, a bright ten-year-old from Etobicoke. He was obviously a go-getter.

He summed up the training from his point of view when he leaned over and told me in a confidential way, "You can still be a patroller without going to the camp. But it sure helps if you want to get ahead in the business. It's the only way to get to be a captain."

World's Champion Songwriter

When we're near Orangeville, we often take a side trip into Hockley Valley. I've always liked that name. It has a ring to it. A country sound.

Hockley Valley isn't too far from a bustling highway, but when you drive down into its rolling hills and forests, the raucous, restless traffic on the highway gradually fades to a rustle and you enter a world of pine, spruce, and poplar. A world of squirrels, rabbits, warblers, and the occasional chattering chickadee interrupt nature's soft murmur to announce your arrival.

George Cook's place is near the bottom of the winding hill going into the valley. George has a rustic-looking house nestled in among the trees. It's surrounded by a yard full of old things. There's battered furniture, used tractors, chairs, saws, and old tires. When he gets around to it, he fixes them up and sells them. That's what he says, anyway. But I've been there a few times, and have yet to see him fixing anything.

Usually you'll find him strumming a guitar or scribbling in a looseleaf notebook. George is a songwriter. A super songwriter. He's written more songs than anyone else in the world!

The last time I talked to him, he had written 34,215 songs. That's history by now. He's in Ripley's and the Guinness Book of Records.

Only a couple of hundred of the songs have been published. But that doesn't matter much to George.

He's a big, bluff man in his 70's who loves life and expresses it in his compulsive urge to write songs. He once turned out 100 songs in one day!

Give him even the ghost of an idea and he'll begin to jot down words for a song. Then he'll pick up his guitar and sing it to a tune that comes to him. It's all very spontaneous.

George is also impulsive. One day when we were saying goodbye out in the cluttered yard, he rushed back into the house, brought out his guitar and roared, "I just thought of a song about you."

Throwing back his head and striking the first chord with a flair, he started to sing "Travellin' Man."

I doubt it will ever become a hit. But as we drove back up the winding hill and out of Hockley Valley, I sat tall in the driver's seat. It's not everyday you have a song written about you.

Taj Mahal

I don't suppose too many people around the province have seen India's famous temple, the Taj Mahal. But many have seen pictures of the beautiful mausoleum that was built by an Indian ruler as a memorial to his wife.

Well, about 20 miles northeast of Toronto up on a hill on a country road near Uxbridge, is Ontario's own Taj Mahal. It's not nearly as big, and it's not a replica, but it's similar to the real thing.

It's called the Foster Memorial Temple and was erected in the mid-thirties by Thomas Foster as a memorial to his wife, and his daughter, who had died at the age of ten.

Foster was born near Uxbridge, eventually became a wealthy businessman, and was Mayor of Toronto at one time.

In his late seventies, he decided to tour the world. One of his stops was India where he saw the Taj Mahal and got the idea of creating a temple something like it, but with a Christian adaptation.

Gould Barton, a retired teacher who lives nearby, remembers Foster bringing over workmen from Europe to build the temple. These skilled craftsmen fashioned it in white limestone with a green dome. There are 12 stained glass windows around the dome. There's also a marble altar that holds the remains of Foster's wife and daughter, and when he died, Foster himself was buried there.

The temple is about 60-feet high, and roughly a mile north of the town.

It's never been clear just what it cost to build, but Foster didn't pull any punches. The limestone alone was worth well over a couple of hundred thousand dollars. It's now valued at about two million.

People driving by do a double take when they spot it. It's not the sort of thing you expect to see on a country road.

Toymaker

Near the village of Stouffville, there's a toymaker of the old school. His name is Paul Simpson. He's not a little old gentleman with tufts of white hair and glasses perched on the tip of his nose. Paul is only in his thirties and he's over six feet tall.

But he does have a twinkle in his eye as he shows you around his toy shop. And the toys he makes are the sort of things a toymaker of yesteryear might have made. They're all of wood and are modelled on toys that enjoyed world popularity anywhere from 50 to 2,000 years ago.

You'll find such things as the Jacob's Ladder, a climbing panda or an acrobat. They're all action toys — you have to do something to make them work. And they all have some historical background.

Simpson is one of a handful of toymakers in the country who is a toy historian along with actually making the toys. You can watch him making a toy or puzzle, and get a running commentary on its origin as well. Not only that, you can browse through his library. He has one of the largest private collections of books about toys that you'll find anywhere.

When I dropped around, he was putting the finishing touches on some cone puppets. Paul was telling me they go back to Elizabethan times. They're whimsical characters that are manipulated by a stick protruding out of the bottom of the cone. A small child can operate them easily.

Another thing about Paul's place is that there are no "Do Not Touch" signs. In fact, he's surprisingly casual about the whole thing. Customers are free to play with toys as much as they like. Maybe that's why he does so well. Adults come in to pick up a toy for a child, start fooling around and end up leaving with a box full. Half of them for themselves.

I could have spent the whole day in that toy shop. I mentioned it to Paul. He shrugged and said it happens all the time. He told me that despite all his research, he's never come up with an explanation as to why toys hold such a fascination for all of us — at any age.

Little Red Schoolhouse

I went back to school at a little red schoolhouse on the outskirts of Mississauga. The school isn't just a museum piece. It's a real school that has reading, writing and 'rithmetic taught to the tune of a real hickory stick wielded by teacher James Potter Esq.

The students come from various Peel County Education Centres and spend a day at the one-room school to find out what it was like in the old days when you and I were young Maggie.

I arrived at the school early. It was a bitterly cold morning. From the schoolroom window, I could see the kids scurrying across an open field as Mr. Potter, pulling mightily on a long rope, rang the bell up on top of the school.

The youngsters, about 7 or 8 years old, were all bundled up. The girls wore long dresses. The boys looked like pictures you see of Huck Finn and Tom Sawyer. Most of them carried lunch pails. Mr. Potter, dressed in a turn-of-the-century outfit, with a frock coat, greeted his charges at the door. He stood there tall and trim, with an iron-fist-in-a-velvet-glove look.

It soon became obvious that Mr. Potter's word was law! There was a piano in the corner. He walked over to it. When Mr. Potter sat down at the piano nobody laughed. They stood up very straight and sang "The Queen."

It was a brand new experience for the young scholars. There was a slate on every desk. Addition and subtraction began. When answers to questions were required, Mr. Potter barked, "Up on your feet Master James! Up on your feet Miss Emily!"

The computer-conscious kids were slightly bewildered by it all until they got the swing of it. Then they loved it. They began to share Mr. Potter's enthusiasm. He scattered praise around when it was due. But a mistake in grammar meant sitting on a stool and wearing a dunce cap!

The school is in a perfect setting. A striking re-creation of the country schools the childrens' grandparents attended. But the focal point is Mr. Potter himself. He's been a teacher since he was 17. He began his career at a one-room school near Rice Lake and has taught for over 50 years. He's considered top-flight in the profession. The school was his idea and the Peel Board went along with it.

He never married, although he says he came close to it a couple of times. Teaching is his life. He's completely devoted to it. They tell me he's the sort of teacher that students never forget. He's invited to weddings, christenings and so on, and at Christmas receives hundreds of cards from former students.

And the secret of successful teaching? Very simple, says Mr. Potter, "Know what you're talking about, and be a damn good actor."

Harry Oakman's "Monarch of the Canadian Wilderness". In 1/500 of a second he hit the jackpot.
photo by: H.R. Oakman

Peterborough Postcard Company

Harry Oakman runs a business from the cluttered basement of his bungalow on a side street in Peterborough. It doesn't appear to be much of a business, but Harry's Peterborough Postcard Company is likely the largest operation of its kind in Canada.

There are over half a million negatives and transparencies in the small basement and the photos have been reproduced on 65 million postcards!

The pictures are all aerial shots, and experts have called Harry Oakman "the best aerial photographer in the world."

Even more surprising is that Oakman's success story hinged on one single picture he took about 30 years ago.

In the early 50's, Harry eked out a living taking aerial pictures of tourist resorts around the Kawartha Lakes. He'd hustle the glossy prints to the resort owners and hopefully get orders for postcards.

Then one day while flying over bush country he swooped down to get a shot of a bull moose swimming in a lake. The roar of the engine startled the moose and he headed for land. As he came out of the water Harry caught the action. In 1/500th of a second Harry Oakman made a fortune!

The picture postcard which became known as "Monarch of the Canadian Wilds" sold in the millions and the blowup hangs in boardrooms from London to Hong Kong.

Harry's business boomed after that. He had salesmen travelling the country taking orders, but saw no reason to change his location. The salesmen were on the road most of the time and his wife Clare, did the books. Printing was farmed out, so the Peterborough Postcard Company just stayed put.

When I first visited the place some years ago, I had a hard time finding it. It was tiny and unimposing. But all the essential equipment was there, including three magnificent custom cameras.

Harry is now in his seventies and works when he feels like it. The last time I saw him, he was at Peterborough's Artspace where his career was outlined in a display of his work and highlights of his adventurous career.

As we wandered around the gallery we talked about the day he took me up in one of his planes so I could get a really good look at his beloved Kawartha Lakes country.

Then we drove over to his bungalow on Cameron Street for a coffee. After awhile we went downstairs to the Peterborough Postcard Company. The company that became famous in 1/500th of a second with a single shot!

The cluttered little basement office hadn't changed a bit.

The Forgotten Chapel

Sometimes you overlook the obvious. Although I've been travelling the province for years I didn't know there was a Royal Chapel of the Mohawks in Eastern Ontario until its Bicentennial was being celebrated. It's located on the Tyendinaga Reserve which surrounds the village of Deseronto.

I made a few inquiries. No one I talked to including a couple of historians, had heard of it either. Yet it's the oldest chapel in Ontario!

Not only that, it's one of just two Royal chapels to exist outside the United Kingdom. The other is the Royal Chapel of the Mohawks in Brantford which has been well publicized.

"The Forgotten Chapel", as I began to think of it, was built in 1774 shortly after some of the Royalist Mohawks landed at the Bay of Quinte following the American Revolution. Led by Chief Deseronto, there were only 15 families up there. They had been granted land by the Crown for their loyalty.

As soon as they landed on Quinte shores they turned over their canoes and held a church service, using their treasured Queen Ann Silver Communion Service.

That's a story in itself. They had received the silver service from Queen Ann when five Mohawk Chiefs went to England in the early 1700's to meet the Queen. They took the present back to their settlement near Fort Hunter in New York state. When the Americans pillaged their villages they buried the silver and dug it up later when they left for Canada.

Shortly after clearing the land near the Bay and establishing what is now Tyenindaga, they built the chapel under royal patronage. There are three pieces of the silver at the chapel. The remainder went with Chief Joseph Brant and a larger band who went on to the Brantford district.

The custodian of the silver at Tyendinaga is Melville Hill, a former chief, a descendant of Deseronto and now the band's historian. He was telling me it's the most historic, the oldest and most valuable silver in Canada.

The Royal Chapel itself is a beautiful little church. The Anglican clergyman, Rev. Kenneth Blaiber, simulated a brief ceremony for us. His official title is "Chaplain of the Mohawks of the Quinte". The choir sang in Mohawk, in the shadow of the Union Jack and the coat of arms sent to the Royal Chapel by George III.

Melville Hill was saying that the chapel has never been visited by royalty, although members of the Royal Family have been to the Brantford Chapel on numerous occasions.

Meanwhile, the loyalist Mohawks continue to hope that someday there will be a Royal Visit to "The Forgotten Chapel".

Merry-Go-Round

If you happen to visit Lakeside Park at Dalhousie, you may notice that something new has been added. Or to be more accurate, something old has been added.

It's a restored merry-go-round. And it's the pride and joy of the St. Catharines parks and recreation people. They run Lakeside and when the city bought the amusement park in 1970 the old carousel was part of the deal. It had been mauled badly by vandals, but there was enough left to put it back into shape. The restoration took three years and it was a labour of love for city employees. The foreman on the job, Pete Bagola, told me the men working on it were so interested they ate their lunch and had coffee breaks right on the spot while discussing their next move.

Peter says none of them knew much about carousels — they just played it by ear. The old merry-go-round was built in 1896. It was one of the only two ever built with four rows of horses, lions and so on.

A lot of work like scraping was done by volunteers and they've all done a wonderful job of restoration. They've also constructed a brick and cement building to house the venerable machine.

I had a more than casual interest in the old merry-go-round. When I was a kid I used to go to Lakeside Park on picnics with my family. We'd go across the lake on "The Northumberland" or "The Dalhousie City". They seemed like ocean liners to me at the time and for a nickel I could ride the merry-go-round when we got to the park.

And y'know, that merry-go-round, the same one, looks better today than when I rode it more than half a century ago!

Len Cullen — Dreamer

The child in us never really goes away, but too often it's covered up by the cares of adulthood. We're so concerned about the past and the future that we forget how to live the present moment — the way children and wise old men and women do.

Cullen Gardens in Whitby brings out the child in you. People walk around with smiles on their faces. They smile as they wander beside the beautiful beds of flowers. They stop and stare with wonder and curiosity at the miniature village in among the gardens. They smile in admiration at the meticulous workmanship it required. They become absorbed in one of the little stores or little people on the main street of the village.

Come to think of it, Len Cullen, the man who created the whole thing, always seems to be smiling too. Maybe it's because he's fulfilled a dream he had 30 years ago. And he did it the hard way. Not much money but lots and lots of dreams.

The result is 23 acres of gardens with 100,000 tulips, crocus and daffodils in the springtime, innumerable plants and flowers during the summer, all surrounded by hundreds more acres of green space and woods.

You can walk and talk with nature in the woods. You might see a rabbit scoot by. There are frogs and toads, trout and goldfish and a long-time resident turtle who likes to play "catch-a-swan." Don't worry, the swan knows his tricks and outsmarts him every time.

On top of that is the miniature Ontario small town. Each one of the

The buildings in Cullen's Miniature Ontario Village are exact replicas of the real ones in various parts of the province.

buildings is an exact replica of a real shop or school or church somewhere in Ontario. The appliance store exists in Cobourg. Anne Tekes Furniture is in Port Hope. The miniatures are accurate right to the number of bricks in the buildings. There are well over 100 buildings, 150 cars and trucks and 600 little people. It took designer Owen Hackey and his crew 14 years to build the tiny town.

Although the showplace closes in October, it's open during the Christmas season and there are twinkling lights everywhere which makes the gardens and town shimmer with colour. It's magic!

The last time I was there at Christmas time, I swear I saw a couple of sugar plum fairies dancing by. Of course, the previous summer I thought I saw Tinkerbell swirling through the air surrounded by fireflies.

Nobody believed me except Len Cullen. And everybody knows he's just a dreamer. But he's also a distributor of dreams. Just ask any of the millions of people who have strolled through his gardens.

Barn-Raising Bee

We went to an old-fashioned barn-raising bee at the hamlet of Vandorf just north of Toronto. It was the first community style barn-raising in that area in 25 years.

But it was nothing new to some of the farmers who were there. They'd worked the land long before Highway 401 cut a swath through the countryside to become Ontario's main street. Long before the city mushroomed out to engulf the fields of grain and pasture.

The event was the first step in the re-creation of a complete family farm at the Whitchurch-Stouffville Museum.

The barn, originally built about 1850, was donated to the museum. It had been carted in pieces from a farm a few miles from Vandorf. By the time everybody arrived for the actual raising, the barn had been pretty well put together.

I didn't see any of the 27 men working on it using nails. The joints were pinned together with wooden pegs. They were telling me that's why old barns lasted so long. They weren't as rigid and gave with the wind.

Before the raising began, the workers were given a typical farm meal. Morley Symes was there. In his day, he built more than 300 barns. Everybody was asking him questions. I guess he was sort of an advisor.

Jim Rae was there. He's raised a lot of barns too and was the work captain on this job. He was telling the others that this would likely be the last barn raising in the district.

Finally everything was ready. We went back out to the barn and people began to gather around it.

Jim Rae started to call out "Heave ... Push." The pike poles were on one side, the ropes on the other. Some of the spectators joined the workers. Slowly, the side of the barn went up.

I got the feeling I was watching something I might never see again. Standing beside me was a wide-eyed boy, about seven years old. I visualized him in years to come telling his grandchildren that way back in the 80's he once saw an old-fashioned barn-raising in a little hamlet called Vandorf.

Muskoka & Southern Georgian Bay

Roughing It

One spring I decided to visit a few of our Provincial Parks - like Killarney and Algonquin. I thought it might be good for the soul. I'd get off the highways, away from the exhaust fumes and go into the wilderness. The spirit would be renewed.

Mind you, it was going to be busman's holiday. I estimated that we could shoot three or four TV news items along the way.

I discussed the project with cameraman Tim Moses, Phil Nolan, our sound technician and my wife Jenny, who as I've mentioned, is a production assistant.

They agreed that a wilderness trip would be a great idea and since they had been spending so much time in the city, it might renew their spirits too.

We planned to rough it. We'd pitch a tent and make a fire by rubbing sticks together or something. We'd fish, gather berries or any other tasty vegetation we could find and live off the land. Then we'd record our experience on videotape, send it back to Global for editing and let Jan Tennant sit there and drool with envy.

Tim would be our guide. He's an outdoorsman. He's also a scuba diver, fisherman, white water canoeist and so on. Besides, Tim had all the equipment - even a canoe. We wouldn't have to rent a thing. Jenny had a few reservations about the project. Of course, in her job she gets stuck with a lot of detail and likes our plans to be as simple as possible.

Anyway, we planned our work and worked our plan. We headed for beautiful Killarney Park on Georgian Bay.

When we arrived, the white quartzite of the La Cloche Mountains gleamed in the sunlight. We grabbed our equipment and packsacks and trudged into the bush. We picked a campsite and Tim showed us how to pitch a tent. Then he took a shot of me in profile looking across the Georgian Bay - like Champlain.

But we ran into a snag. Up to this point none of us had complained about the blackflies or mosquitoes. It would have shown weakness. We sweated it out. Phil, however, who's a quiet type as befits a good sound man, had been taking a bad beating from the blackflies. His face was starting to puff up. Then his arms. Soon he looked like the Pillsbury Doughboy!

We got out of there fast. We backtracked along the trail, loaded the cars with our gear and took off for Killarney Village a few miles away. On the outskirts we spotted a posh hotel which turned out to be Killarney Mountain Lodge, described in its brochure as "an oasis of comfort in the wilderness". We needed it.

We got some stuff for Phil's puffed-up face, had a swim in the heated pool and over a splendid dinner in the rustic dining room considered our next move.

Jenny suggested that we postpone the venture until later in the summer...or perhaps in the fall...or even next winter when we could do a snow story. No one objected. We agreed that the idea had been a good one - we just didn't get the breaks.

A few hours later we were back on Highway 401. Back to the rat race. Back home.

Backstage at Ste. Marie

You may be one of the two million or more people who have visited Ste. Marie Among the Hurons, a few miles from the Georgian Bay town of Midland. It's a reconstruction of Ontario's first European settlement that French colonists, Hurons and Jesuits established in the wilderness in 1639.

There are 22 buildings in the community and the young people portraying labourers, priests and craftsmen make it all seem very authentic.

And Ste. Marie is authentic. Archaeologists studied the site for years and then went to work. The job was completed in 1968 and historians, tourists and school children began to pour in to experience life in a different century.

One day I dropped in on a few of the artists and artisans behind the scenes at Ste. Marie. People who live in the surrounding area.

In nearby Victoria Harbour, I watched Raymond DesChenes creating authentic candlesticks of Renaissance design for the Ste. Marie Chapel. Ray has been a restorer of fine art and wood for more than three decades and has been a valuable asset to Ste. Marie for years. A scholar as well as an artist, he has a library of 3,000 books for reference.

A few miles away at a little shop called "Grass Roots" in the village of Wyebridge, Trish Hines weaves many of the costumes for the "Jesuits" who roam the site. When I arrived, she was weaving another of the "black robes." Ten yards of material are needed for each cassock, stretching 60 inches in width when woven on the loom.

Trish estimates it takes about 60 hours to weave the material for a robe, and she limits herself to four hours a day "or else I would be seeing a chiropractor every day."

In a workshop close to the Ste. Marie palisades, carpenter Elmer LeClair of Midland was working on the base of a beautiful tabernacle. Elmer is an expert in the wood-making skills of three centuries ago.

I've been going to Ste. Marie since the first archaeologists were sifting through the rubble. But it wasn't until years later that I saw some of the artists and artisans from the surrounding area at work. Through their skills, more than two million visitors have experienced a link with the 17th century. A link with our heritage.

Birdman of Bala

When in the Muskoka district, I sometimes visit Jim Tilley and his homing pigeons. Ever since I met him some years ago, I've always thought of Jim as "The Birdman of Bala."

Jim and his wife are year-round residents of the beautiful little town and like others who live there, they wouldn't budge from Bala. Besides, Jim has his racing pigeons. It's their home too.

There were over 60 pigeons the last time I was there. They live in a loft behind the Tilleys' bungalow which is just down the road from the O.P.P. offices where Jim was a maintenance man before he retired.

It's hard to say how many pigeons Jim has cared for over the years. It's a hobby that began when he was a boy of ten and he's never lost interest in it. I guess Jim has had some pretty speedy pigeons. The Tilleys' living room is packed with trophies dating back to 1935.

Jim was one of the founders of the Orillia Homing Pigeon Club. Like other clubs, they have weekly races, transporting the pigeons to distant points in Ontario and then setting them free.

The club members have ingenious maps and timing devices which enable the judges to pick the winners. Obviously, the pigeons have different destinations. They have just one objective: to return to their own roosts as quickly as possible. When a pigeon arrives home and enters the roost, it sets off a small sealed timer. The timer is then sent to the judges. The system is foolproof.

The Birdman of Bala is an expert on homing pigeons. He can tell you innumerable stories about famous pigeons in history and how the birds were man's messengers for centuries.

But even Jim doesn't know why they have such a compulsion to return home.

"It's possible," he says, "that they want to get back to their mates and offspring."

Whatever it is, they'll battle hawks, hail, rain, and winds to get back to their base. And most of the time they make it.

Scoots

If you've been to the Georgian Bay area in wintertime, you may have seen "scoots." They're speedy, noisy craft that look like a punt and have small airplane engines on the back.

They're the forerunners of the snowmobile. But unlike snowmobiles, they are amphibious. And they've been around the Bay for over half a century.

One January, I was taking a coffee break at a truck stop on the highway south of Parry Sound, when Jim McKinnon, a woodsman buddy of mine, pulled in. He was on his way back to pick up a scoot that B.B. Robitaille had made for him.

B.B. Robitaille (nobody seems to know his first name) is one of those few, hardy camp keepers who live year-round in the ruggedly beautiful 20,000 Islands area of Southern Georgian Bay. The "keepers" take care of the exclusive clubs and big summer homes during the winter.

I mentioned to Jim that although I'd been on just about every other kind of boat and sled, I'd never had a ride on a scoot.

An hour later, we were at a dock on Twelve Mile Lake where Jim's partner, Bob Garratt, was waiting with a scoot to take us over to the Tadanac Club where B.B. looks after things.

Bob had his scoot going. It was a modern version with a hull of fibreglass. But with the regular rebuilt small airplane engine.

We took off over the ice, shouting to one another above the roar of the engine. I saw a patch of open water in the distance. As we approached it, Bob slowed down. We hit the water and the scoot made the switch easily. Thirty seconds later we were up again, skimming over the ice.

When we arrived at the Tadanac Club, Joe Reynolds was there. He's the keeper at Iron City, a nearby club that sportsmen from Pittsburg frequent in the summer. He'd come over to visit B.B. Robitaille. Predictably, he came in his scoot.

I discovered that camp keepers swear by their scoots. They're the only machines they trust in that part of Georgian Bay. And I can see why. Even in the dead of winter there are open patches of water due to the currents caused by the howling northwest winds.

I suggested that the original notion for the scoot might have come from the type of craft used in the Florida Everglades.

On the contrary. It turns out the Florida people got the idea from the camp keepers of Georgian Bay many years ago.

Canada's Purest Water

Cool, clear water is becoming scarce these days. But there's plenty of it in the Southern Georgian Bay town of Penetanguishene. It's the home of "Canada's Purest Water." It says so on a big billboard at the entrance to the town.

The billboard has been there since I was a Boy Scout, and used to go up that way to summer camp. I never thought to ask just why the water was the purest in the country. None of us did. The billboard said it all.

Later on, I learned that there are artesian wells scattered throughout the area.

The only person I know who ever challenged the "purest water" was Jim Petrie of Orr Lake. That's about 10 miles south of Penetanguishene on Highway 93.

If you happen to drive through the tiny community you'll notice what Jim calls "The Fabulous Fountain of Orr Lake."

Jim used to run a service station on the highway, until he sold it a few years ago. The fountain is right beside the service station and was included in the sale.

It's quite a fountain. Jim built a sort of pyramid of whiskey barrels around it and artesian well water gushes up into the air at the rate of 60 gallons a minute! But here's the thing. Jim says it's the purest water you can find anywhere. So where does that leave Penetanguishene? I mentioned this to Jim. He brushed off the idea.

"Penetang's water is all right," said Jim, "but you can't beat this water. It's as pure as the driven snow." I tested it. It's free and there's no question it's world class. It's cool, clear and refreshing.

But I still have a soft spot in my heart for Penetanguishene's water. One reason, I guess, is its long-standing reputation. And when you've had that slogan "Canada Purest Water" rammed down your throat since you were a Boy Scout, it's hard to keep an open mind.

Another reason is that we have a tree farm about five miles from Penetanguishene. When we're not on the road we go up there to sniff the Georgian Bay air and walk in the woods.

We have good well water, but every once in a while we go over to the town to get the really good stuff out of an old beat-up tap near the water works!

That's right! That's all there is - an old beat-up tap. No signs! No indication that the water is famous! Nothing! I mentioned this to the Mayor. He says they're working on it. They're going to pave the area, and put pines in the background. They're going to dress it up. Maybe next year.

They don't push it in Penetang. They move in a pretty easygoing way. In this case, they'll go with the flow.

Cranberry Farm

One autumn I went up to Gibson Reserve in Muskoka to take a look at the cranberry harvest which was just getting underway.

There are only two cranberry farms in Ontario. One is a few miles north of Bala, which musician Orville Johnston has operated as a sideline for the past 25 years.

A larger one, at a reserve, was started by the Iroquois band over a decade ago. It's become quite an operation, employing 28 band members during peak periods and turning out well over a quarter million pounds of berries every year.

Bud Rennie, who was born on the reserve, has been the manager since the project started. He showed me around the 30-acre farm.

Cranberries don't grow on bushes. They grow on vines close to the ground and they have to be watched like babies from May to harvest time in October. A lot of things can happen to them.

The Iroquois have built canals between the beds. At harvest time control gates are released and the berries float to the surface. Then they are beaten off the vines by special machines which are driven through the water. The machines whack away at the berries with paddle wheels.

The cranberries are boomed to a corner of the canal and picked up by conveyors which tumble them into a hopper. Then they are taken to a nearby barn where they are dried, sorted and bagged. Finally, they are carted by truck to processors in the city.

It was raining cats and dogs the day I was there, but everybody kept on working - apparently time is a precious commodity when you're harvesting cranberries.

The whole thing appeared to me to be a very straightforward operation. I asked Bud what could go wrong. He turned and stared at me - somewhat incredulously.

"What can go wrong?" he shouted. "Just about anything when you are fighting nature — frost, drought, bugs, hail..."

He went on and on. I stood there in the pouring rain and listened - shifting from one foot to another.

I ended up with a five-pound bag of cranberries and a bad cold.

Marine Railway

Even if you've lived in Ontario all your life, it's quite possible that you've never heard of a tourist attraction that draws visitors from all over the world.

It's the massive marine railway near Severn Falls about 20 miles northeast of Orillia. It's a 110-ton cradle of steel that hauls boats up and down a steep hill at the Georgian Bay end of the Trent-Severn Waterway.

The railway was built recently to replace a smaller one that had been in service since 1917. Over the years, millions of people came to take a look at the first one. But the new mechanical monster dwarfs it.

People are fascinated by the big fella as it lumbers up and down the hill, carrying cruisers and sailboats. It's 80-feet long and 24-feet wide. The pulleys that yank it up and ease it down are connected to four powerful engines.

I went up to see it when they completed it in the late seventies. They had a lot of trouble with it the first year. The thing just wouldn't work properly and the smaller railway still had to carry the boats. Sailors were saying the incredible hulk was a five-million-dollar white elephant.

But they got the kinks out of it and now it's doing a great job. It handles about 12,000 boats in a season and each year an estimated 165,000 tourists visit the installation.

Mike LeDuc, the lockmaster, was telling me the reason for setting up the original railway years ago was to keep the lampreys from swimming from Georgian Bay into Lake Simcoe. However, he says the government likely figured it would also become a mecca for tourists.

That's what happened. The Kodak Company says the most photographed attraction in Canada is still Niagara Falls. But do you know what's second? Ontario's big marine railway!

Shutterbugs love it! After all, it's the only one of its kind in the whole world.

The Magic of Muskoka

I like to mosey around Muskoka any time of year. Sometimes I stop at Sloan's in Gravenhurst for a coffee and renew acquaintance with old Press Club cronies like Strathy Smith, Jack Hutton or Hugh Clairmont.

Hugh and his trumpet have become something of a tradition in Muskoka. The day the restored "Segwun," the venerable steamer, began sailing the lakes again, Hugh with trumpet and straw hat was standing on the bow playing Dixieland.

When the Bethune homestead was officially opened, Hugh was there. So was Hollywood's Otto Preminger, gathering material for a movie about Canada's famous Dr. Bethune who was so beloved by the Chinese.

Although the big season in Muskoka is summertime, the "Cavalcade of Colour" in the autumn runs it a close second. Most of us don't realize that the changing leaves up through Bracebridge, Huntsville, Bala, and beyond is a world-class event. There are few places anywhere that compare with the spectacle.

But Muskoka is also a beautiful district in winter. I like to go up to High Falls near Bracebridge where David and Mary Brooks live. David is with Natural Resources and puts me on to all sorts of wildlife stories.

I'm always wondering how the deer are doing during the winter months and David makes arrangements for me to get out to the deer-yards - clearings where the deer gather to feed.

We wait for a heavy snowfall and when it clears I join one of the government crews on their regular runs.

Early in the morning, they put snowmobiles, snowshoes and bags of feed on trucks and head for the yards.

The deer need help in the winter. Aside from trying to escape the natural predators, they have a hard time getting food in the deep snow. The crews cut the browse that is beyond their reach and leave it for them. Then they put grain in feeders to supplement the deer's diet.

It's an annual outing I look forward to. As I trudge on snowshoes across the crisp snow in among the pines, I'm keenly aware of the magic of Muskoka.

Red Baron

It was one of those clear, crisp winter days in Muskoka. The branches of the pines and spruce were heavily laden with snow that sparkled in the sunbeams. I trudged along a trail through bush country trying to follow Otto Roosen who would stop periodically and wait for me to catch up. Roosen, although crowding 90 at the time, had the agility and stamina of a youngster!

I had arrived at his home near Utterson earlier that morning to see his paintings and hear about his past. But it was such a beautiful day, I suggested we go for a walk first. I thought he'd just shuffle along, the way most 90-year-old people do. I miscalculated badly. I discovered that Otto walked with the speed of a cross-country skier. Or so it seemed to me. We finally arrived back at his house that's set among the pines in the Lake Rosseau area and I sank into the nearest armchair.

Otto lives alone. He goes into nearby Huntsville occasionally to get supplies, but on most days he's at his easel painting from sunrise to dusk. His paintings are everywhere around the house. Hundreds of them. Mostly of the wildlife that abounds in Muskoka. He loves the birds and the animals he often sees right around his home.

But there's another side to Otto Rossen. I'd heard about it from

Otto's friend "The Red Baron" being decorated in 1917. Otto's friends are now the World War I Canadian pilots he has met since coming to Canada.
photo by: O. Roosen

Andy Hamilton of Brantford who is interested in aviation history and some of the early pilots who helped make it.

Roosen was a German flying ace during World War 1, was a friend of the Red Baron, Manfried von Richtofen, and had three planes shot out from under him. One of them by Canada's Billy Bishop!

Historian Hamilton arranged to have Roosen meet Tommy Williams of Woodstock, at that time the oldest surviving Canadian fighter pilot of World War 1. Tommy had written a book about his experiences and gave Roosen a copy with the inscription "To my former enemy, now my friend." It was an historic meeting the likes of which may never occur again. Such flyers are a diminishing breed.

I spent the day with Roosen. Listened as he spun tales of the Red Baron and of the day Billy Bishop swooped down from behind a cloud, shot down two German planes and a balloon before hitting Roosen's plane and forcing him to the ground.

Otto is quite willing to poke into the past, but seems more interested in talking about the present and the things he is painting. By the way, none of his paintings are for sale. He's had them in shows and is delighted to let visitors see them, but he says those birds and animals in the paintings have become his friends. And he doesn't want to part with them.

Bygone Days Farm

Not too far from Collingwood there's a little village. You won't find it on any map, and only two people live there. But they have a lot of friends. School children visit them. Senior citizens visit them. A lot of people like to visit them. It's a pioneer village - with a difference. It was started in the late sixties by Frank and Shirley Fisher as a retirement project.

The Fishers had raised their family on a large market gardening spread in Islington. They sold it to a developer in the late fifties and became financially independent. For awhile they lived in the city, but missed farm life.

One day when they were out for a drive up around Collingwood, they saw a farm for sale. On the way home they got an idea. They'd go back farming in the old-fashioned way and also build their own pioneer village around it!

They bought the farm, got a few cows, pigs, chickens, geese and a horse. Then they started a big garden. They lived off the land, more or less, and decided to call the place Bygone Days Farm.

The first building they bought for the village itself was a church that had been built in 1880 and was about to be demolished. Transporting it was a problem but they managed to truck it over from nearby Dundalk.

Later, they acquired a schoolhouse of 1879 vintage. One thing led to another and now they have six early houses of different constructions and 13 business establishments - among them a blacksmith shop and a sawmill.

The Fishers are the busiest, happiest couple you ever saw. They're up early in the morning doing chores and spend the day working around the village. On Sundays, they dress in old-time outfits and greet visitors. Both of them act as guides, explaining how things were done in the old days.

And how much does it cost to build your own pioneer village? Well, here's how the Fishers put it:

"Instead of a trip to Hawaii, we bought a schoolhouse. Instead of a Cadillac, we bought a steam engine."

They like it that way. To Frank and Shirley Fisher it's The Good Life.

Old Organs

Back in the days when a living room was called a parlour and life was less complicated, families used to gather around the parlour organ and listen to or sing the old songs.

You can still see parlour organs in pioneer villages or heritage houses. Most of the time they don't work. They just sit there among the vintage furniture and the whole thing is roped off so visitors won't harm anything.

But recently I saw a collection of parlour organs that made me gasp in admiration. They've been gathered and completely restored by Ernie Nicholson, a retired businessman in the Georgian Bay town of Midland.

It's thought to be the largest collection of restored organs in the country. There are 20 of them. And all of them work!

Ernie says he could write a book about each one of them. All were dilapidated derelicts. He picked them up in cow stables, driving sheds, at auction sales and from scrap heaps.

For the past 20 or so years Ernie has scrounged around for parts, replaced decayed wood, repaired pedals. In some cases, he has laboured in his basement workshop for over a year restoring a single organ. After all, some of the beautifully crafted instruments are well over 100 years old.

Although Ernie restores them, it's his wife Islay who plays them, along with eight of her friends. Some years ago they formed a local organ club.

I watched them in action at Nicholson's home on Hugel Avenue. They played nine of the organs in unison. The strains of "When You and I were Young, Maggie " echoed around the house and for a few cherished moments we all relived the days of our early childhood.

The Hidden Talents

If you ever get a chance to see "The Hidden Talents" don't miss them. They're a musical group with a twist. They're all priests!

I met them as they were rehearsing for a show in Huntsville. Appropriately, there are twelve in the group. They're young and full of fun. They have musical talent to burn and wherever they go they play to packed halls and theatres. A sellout every time!

They came from various parishes in the Roman Catholic diocese of Sault Ste. Marie and do about six shows a year for charity.

On stage, wearing sweaters and jeans, they could be a bunch of men going on a fishing trip. Not a white collar in sight.

They play and sing everything from hits of the twenties to the classics. They bubble with enthusiasm. Kid each other. Kid the audience. They interrupt a solo by suddenly breaking into close harmony. Or one of them will take off and do the Charleston. The audience rocks with laughter.

For the first half of the program there isn't a smidgen of religion. But in the second half they switch to music of a more spiritual nature, but never really lose the lighter touch.

The manager of "The Hidden Talents" is Father Greg Humbert of Espanola. He laughs a lot and reminds me of Robin Hood's Friar Tuck.

"Something magical happens at the concerts," he said. "People relate to us differently. They see our human side. It's good for us and good for them."

The priests are all trained musicians. Before being ordained most of them played in clubs, cabarets or pubs.

They describe their music as "songs we learned at our mother's knee, and other joints."

"The Hidden Talents" in a formal photo. When they're on stage the picture changes.

Steamer Clark

If you live around Collingwood, you've likely heard of Steamer Clark. His real name is Gordon but people in the area have called him "Steamer" for years.

He became interested in machinery when he was six years old. He used to hang around a machine shop and says he's been "hooked" on machinery ever since.

He worked as a machinist at Collingwood Shipyards for 40 years and along the line became an expert in steam engines. Some of his former shipyard buddies go farther than that. One of them told me that Steamer is a "genius" with machinery.

Tourists know about him because of his steamboat. He berths it down on Georgian Bay, which is about a mile from his house.

When I went over to see him, he was laying up the boat for the winter. It's a 30-foot steel-hulled craft that he built from scratch after he retired from the shipyards.

Steamer is now about 75, but the way he was hopping around the steamboat, he could have been a teenager. He's lean and little, with energy to burn.

He was also building another steamboat. It's a 40-foot job. He's built two engines for it. He doesn't know which one to use. He hasn't made up his mind.

We went down to his basement workshop. I'd heard about the basement. Steamer has built just about everything in it from scrap metal. From scratch - like the boats. He built the wood-burning furnace, the hot water heater and the lathe where he does most of his work.

He showed me the new engines. One of them gives him the option of converting to a semi-diesel type of operation. The other is a compound steam engine. He'll likely put one of them into a steam tractor he plans to make.

He explained the differences in the engines. I nodded wisely, but I had no idea of what he was talking about. I lost him after the first ten seconds.

Where does he find the time to do these things? He starts his day at 8 a.m. and finishes about 1 a.m. Then he'll have a lunch and be in bed by 2:30 in the morning. He says he can hardly wait to get up so he can get going on his various projects.

There's no question he's a mastermind with machinery. But what impresses you even more is his enthusiasm for living. He may be in his seventies but he still has the heart of that six-year-old boy who got "hooked" on machines many years ago.

The Severn Bird Farm

Moving day is a chore for anybody. Getting all your stuff packed and moved to another country is still worse. But moving your family plus a thousand or more valuable birds is a challenge that would shake the serenity of a saint. Especially when you're moving them from West Germany to Ontario!

Yet Friedhelm and Birgit Hoesterey are a knowledgeable young German couple who are doing it. They set up a bird farm at Severn Bridge north of Orillia and managed to bring about 150 birds. But moving all of them to their new home is going to take at least five years!

It's because of the strict regulations involved in bringing birds from another country. They're allowed to transport just three or four small shipments a year. When they do arrive, the birds are quarantined for up to 45 days in a special barn about a mile away from the farm.

Most of the birds are endangered species and all were born in captivity. The couple breed and sell birds, and the farm is an educational centre for schoolchildren, tourists and naturalists.

Friedhelm has been interested in birds since he was a boy. Hang around with him for a few hours and you'll learn a lot about birds. As we walked near the cages he told me about the habits of his East European Hawks and falcons, Lenner falcons from Africa, Harris Hawks from Texas and European eagle owls, which are the world's largest. The exotic birds are housed in a separate area.

Apparently, there's a big market for birds these days, with city apartment dwellers the big buyers. Friedhelm and Birgit say they have the only farm in the province devoted exclusively to birds. But as they say, the best is yet to come. Most of their birds are still in West Germany being cared for by friends who are also in the business.

So their extended moving day is going to be a long haul -with a cargo that flaps and flutters.

Missing the Boat

Early one spring I boarded a Canadian Coastguard icebreaker at the dock of the Georgian Bay town of Midland. In the mad March days, the icebreakers have plenty to do.

I had a hard time locating the icebreakers. We couldn't make connections. There were two of them in the area. They were coming and going. They were out cutting channels and going into ports around southern Georgian Bay to free the big freighters from their prisons of ice.

I managed to find the "Griffon" one day. It was berthed at the town dock and I made arrangements to go out the next morning. We had it all set up. But overnight things changed. The "Griffon" had to go to Owen Sound unexpectedly. They left a message that the "Montmorency," the other icebreaker, would be at nearby Port McNicol. I rushed over there but the "Montmorency" was just pulling away after releasing a lakeboat at the grain elevators. I had missed the boat again.

I phoned the regional headquarters in Toronto. I talked to Daisy Morant who handles public relations for the Coastguard. She said I was bound to find an icebreaker down in Port Colborne where the ice was heavy. She said she would arrange everything. I was to call the next day. I called, but Daisy had the flu and couldn't be reached.

A week passed. Most of the lakeboats had gone out. It looked as if I wasn't going to make it.

I was disappointed. It's become an annual tradition for me to get out on an icebreaker. To watch the sturdy vessels ride up on the stubborn ice and break it with their weight. To hear the crunch and crackle. To see the ice float away in pieces. To stand at the stern of the ship and see the ribbon of open water getting longer and longer. To me, it's a sure sign of Spring. Like seeing the sap running again, or the first robin.

I was ready to leave the area but drove down to the town dock for a final look. I couldn't believe it. There was the "Montmorency"!

I parked the car and ran over to the gangplank. They saw me coming and took me to see the young captain, Mark Taylor.

I told him my sad story. He shook his head slowly in sympathy. He was sorry, he said, but his ship was heading for Collingwood.

I explained that my trip was traditional, but I didn't have time to go to Collingwood. Captain Taylor looked thoughtful. Then he picked up the phone and made a few fast calls.

He didn't fool around. Ten minutes later the "Montmorency" cast off.

I stood on the bridge with the Captain. The "Montmorency" rode over the remaining ice that was making a last stand. I heard the crunch and the crackle. We didn't stay out very long. But it was my own personal voyage, and for me, Spring had arrived!

As they dropped me off at the town dock, I thanked young Captain Taylor. That's what I like about seafaring men. They're strong on tradition.

The Tale of Two Turtles

A few years ago, I met a couple of turtles named Bill and Emmy at the Wye Marsh Wildlife Centre near Midland. They were unusual in that they were of the relatively rare Blanding species. They both were in the broadcasting business, so we had a lot in common. You'll see what I mean.

On the surface, the Wye Marsh is a tranquil place with birds, small animals, beautiful nature trails and an underwater window at one point. But beneath the surface, it's a seething mass of activity as insects, reptiles and other little critters go about making a living the way nature intended. There's no unemployment down there. Everybody has a job to do.

And interesting things go on at the Wye Marsh - in a quiet way. For example, there was no fanfare, or trumpets, or headlines the day Bill and Emmy were fitted with radio transmitters and sent into the Marsh so they could relay information back to the biologists. The fact that they were believed to be the first underwater creatures to be wired for sound went virtually unnoticed by the press!

However, this was my kind of story. I called it "The Tale of Two Turtles." You can have your assignments in London, Paris, the Mideast, the Far East, Wonga-Wonga and all those other hot spots. Give me a yarn like the travels of Bill and Emmy and I'm really ready to roll!

The rest is now history. Biologist Bert van Ingen, who was in charge of the project, followed the progress of the pair with a special receiving set. He traced their travels on an aerial map. When I went back the next year, Bert reported that Bill Blanding had gone over two miles! Considered an incredible journey for a turtle. But they hadn't heard from Emmy and Bert figured it might be faulty equipment.

Meanwhile, word got around. People started to inquire about Bill's location and would ask to hear his "beep." Bill became the only turtle in the world with his own radio show! He became a star! Made it in show business! Mind you, the ratings weren't outstanding, but there was a faithful audience for "The Bill Blanding Show."

The next year, there was joy in the camp! Emmy not only returned, but laid eggs in a tank when she arrived. Bert was right. Emmy's transmitter was faulty. Bert got some new, improved equipment and added another member to the cast of the show. He's a big snapper called "Fang."

If you visit the Marsh, ask to hear the show. Children love it. They put on headsets and their eyes sparkle when they hear the now-familiar "Beep." Bert, the producer, doesn't expect any further foul-ups! If they do occur, technical problems will be temporary. Please do not adjust your set.

Heat from Peat

I'd never thought much about peat until I started to slosh around in a bog near Parry Sound with Professor Norman Radforth. Dr. Radforth is an expert on peat. A vibrant man in his early seventies with a Santa Claus type beard, he's been studying peat for close to half a century. In fact, he created the classification system for peat.

He's also a consultant for a team of researchers taking an inventory of how much peat is available in Canada. The government wants to know if it's possible to use peat as a low cost fuel.

The team sends aerial photos of bogs located in various parts of the country to Dr. Radforth and he sends back a report on the peat potential in certain areas. Survey teams then send ground samples which he identifies in the laboratory of his rambling home on the outskirts of Parry Sound.

But Dr. Radforth has moved ahead on his own to develop a product called "Peat Heat." It comes in compressed peat bricks that he says have a higher energy content than the best wood. A company has been formed to market the product with the peat coming from bogs around Parry Sound.

With Field Manager Mike Thompson leading the way we went out to see where Professor Radforth's newest baby was born. And that's how I happened to be sloshing around in a bog. It turned out to be a pretty old baby. Maybe about 3,000 years old, and some of the peat in the district is 10,000 years old or more.

I learned something else about bogs. They're tricky. You don't see the holes. What looks like nice solid foliage hides a two-foot hole. Even an old pro like Dr. Radforth fell into one. I was lucky. They steered me away from the bad spots.

Mike reached way down into the moist ground and brought up a fistful of peat. Brownish gooey stuff. "There are 17 different types of peat," said Dr. Radforth, taking a bit of the stuff from Mike's hand. "This type is excellent for energy." He went on to tell me how they dig ditches, drain off the moisture and extrude the peat into four-inch bricks.

"In some European countries, they've been using peat for heat for hundreds of years," he said. "Ireland now generates 25% of it's electricity from peat," he added.

As we trudged back to the highway, I was thinking that some of those old fossils just below the surface of the bog must be pretty hot stuff. Which all goes to prove that there's no fuel like an old fuel.

Maple Syrup

Shortly after the sap started to run, we went over to Elmvale to visit a sugar bush. Elmvale is about 15 miles north of Barrie and one of Ontario's big maple syrup areas.

Just as you approach the village, there's a road leading to what could be called "Maple Syrup Row."

Ken Ritchie's bush, the Greenlaw's and Herman Lalonde's bushes are all located down the road within a few miles of each other.

A group of schoolchildren and their teachers were just pulling into the Lalonde place and cameraman Terry Culbert suggested we go in there so he could get a few good action shots.

My wife Jenny had no real preference as to which camp we went to. But she had that glint in her eye that indicated that wherever we went, she hoped to latch on to some maple syrup to take back with us.

Herman Lalonde and his son Tim greeted us and began showing us around.

It's a traditional bush. There are over 3,000 taps to take care of, and since the sugaring-off season lasts only six weeks or so, they have to keep hopping.

As in most commercial operations these days, the trees are attached by tubing. At Lalonde's the sap is pumped to the holding tanks by a converted milking machine. Herman says it allows him to get 17% more sap. It's just one of the tricks he's picked up in his 50 years in the business!

But there's no Fancy Dan stuff. There's just one evaporator and it's entirely wood-stocked. It takes a cord a day to keep it burning.

Nevertheless, Lalonde and his son had turned out more than 300 gallons when we were there, and that was only halfway into the season.

Jenny and Herman got along fine. She's a farmer's daughter and talks the lingo. And she was all smiles when she got a couple of litres of maple syrup as a present. You'd think she'd been given the Golden Fleece. Of course, at today's prices, maybe the syrup was worth as much as the Golden Fleece.

But you know, scientists still can't figure out how the maple trees do it. Forestry experts are a bit embarrassed about it all.

Why, out of 120 species of maple trees, does only one species manufacture the right sugar? And how do the "vessels" of the trees get filled up and recharged with sugar overnight? Not just once, but day after day throughout the season.

Nobody knows. It's another of those sweet mysteries of life.

Bill getting a few tips about the business from veteran sugar bush operator Herman Lalonde.
photo by: T. Culbert

Budd Watson

Tourists visiting the historic Huronia district consider Ste. Marie Among the Hurons, the Naval and Military Establishments, the Indian village, and Martyrs' Shrine as a "must" on their itinerary.

But if you're up that way in the future, add another one to your list - The Budd Watson Gallery.

It's something you'd expect to find in a metropolitan centre but it's located just off the main street in the town of Midland.

It's a gallery of Watson's own photography, and thought to be the largest privately owned gallery of its kind on the continent.

Watson is a Midland boy whose family has operated a photography studio there for years. He grew up in the business. Eventually, he became interested in landscapes with emphasis on rugged Georgian Bay scenery.

During the past 20 years he's won international acclaim and his pictures hang in public buildings and in boardrooms across Canada and abroad.

A couple of years ago, Budd bought Midland's old YMCA building and converted it into a gallery. It's a big rambling structure. There must be at least 20 big rooms in it and Watson's work is tastefully displayed in most of them. The prices for the pictures range from a hundred to ten thousand dollars.

Part of the building is partitioned off for developing and enlarging. I watched him pulling off a massive six by ten foot print of a scene reminiscent of a Group of Seven painting.

Incidentally, Watson is the only photographer anywhere whose work has been shown at the famed McMichael Gallery at Kleinburg. And it's been said that what the Group of Seven is to painting, Budd Watson is to photography.

He's constantly on the move, teaching and travelling, but he still makes Midland his home.

A classic example of "Local Boy Makes Good."

The spirit of photographer Budd Watson's devotion to the Georgian Bay area is captured in this photo of him taken by one of his students.
photo by: Dr. W. Stavraky

Bigwin Inn

You may have heard of the fabulous Bigwin Inn. When it opened in 1920, it dwarfed all of the other resorts in Muskoka. It was the ultimate in elegance and splendour - smack in the middle of wilderness!

Paul and Rosemary Tapley, who own the Bondi Lodge near Dorset, took me over by boat to Bigwin Island to see what remains of the famous showplace. Its deserted grandeur has gone and many of the floors have buckled. For some reason a grand piano still stands in the rotunda. Mice have nested in it. The place is ghostly - eerie.

But the legend of Bigwin remains. Built by C.O. Shaw, an eccentric entrepreneur, it was designed as a playground for the rich, the powerful and the famous. It could accommodate 500 guests and there were 500 employees to serve them. People came by boat, by train, by plane. The guests included Queen Juliana, The Rockefellers, Clark Cable and Carole Lombard. Big name bands played in the magnificent pavilion. Continental chefs prepared gourmet dishes. The works!

Paul was saying that the decline and fall of Bigwin was due to changing managements and changing times. But the people of Muskoka had never seen such gracious, luxurious living and those that were around during the heyday of the resort still tell endless stories about it.

Bigwin was at its best during the twenties and thirties. But now, it's as if the Great Gatsby, the cast and film crew, wrapped it up, packed their bags and moved away - leaving nothing but a deserted movie set.

Northern Ontario

Harry's Chateau

The main street of Kirkland Lake is paved with gold. You can't see it, but it's there. A construction crew made a mistake. They put down gold ore instead of gravel and covered it with concrete.

It's just one of the scads of tidbits oldtimers toss at you to make Kirkland Lake a newsman's Nirvana.

It's a mining town that's somehow contrived to retain the lusty spirit of the boom years of the 20's and 30's in the goldfields of Northern Ontario.

Colourful characters still roam the streets. They meet in bars and restaurants. They talk of slopes, stopes and shafts. They talk of racing to the recording office after staking their claims. Sometimes winning, sometimes losing.

We met Charlie Chung Chow, who runs "Charlie's Hotel." They told us the dingy bar hasn't changed much since Charlie's father opened it during prohibition days. "Chief" Johnston, the one-man police force used to walk by the hotel playing his beloved bagpipes to warn of the liquor inspector's arrival. That also gave the druggist time to drain his soda-pop machine of booze. And it gave the "blind pigs" like Black Mary's and the Bucket of Blood a chance to make a fast switch.

One old-timer knew prospector Rosa Brown, the town's uncouth Mammy Yokum, who bought up real estate, and with her pack of mangy dogs was the scourge of politicians, tax collectors and bureaucrats.

They're all part of the legend. In one of the store windows we noticed posters of Rosa, her buddy, Sandy McIntyre and Sir Harry Oakes made by Kirkland kids.

It was the Harry Oakes' story that had taken us to Kirkland Lake in the first place. The town's mayor, Joe Mavrinac, a knowledgeable go-getter and Bill Mackie, publisher of "The Northern News," had invited us up to take a look at the Harry Oakes' Museum.

The Museum is packed with artifacts and photos that trace the career of the young prospector who arrived in Kirkland Lake with $2.65 in his pocket and became Canada's richest man after he discovered and developed the fabulous Lake Shore Mine. Along the line, he made a few timely financial contributions to England and was awarded a knighthood. It was a career that ended tragically on July 8, 1943 when he was murdered in his Bahamas mansion in a still unsolved crime.

The Museum is housed in Harry's "chateau" as it was called. It's a 30-room rustic place and there's gold under it!

Miners were down there digging it out. Mayor Joe arranged to have us don miners' outfits and go down to watch the drilling. Then he took us to see the $30 million shaft at Macassa Mines and out to see open pit gold mining a few miles from town.

Joe also introduced us to a couple of rugged-looking prospectors who promised to take us into the bush and show us how to stake a claim.

I got the impression that the somewhat scruffy pair had been kicking around Kirkland Lake for years getting a grubstake here and there.

Later when I mentioned this to Joe, he started to chuckle. "Looks are deceiving around here," he said. "They're both millionaires."

Bush Pilot

People in Sudbury chuckle when they see Rusty Blakey riding to work on his bicycle. He doesn't like driving a car or even riding in one if he can avoid it. A rather small, thin, elderly man, he pedals along to his office looking very much like a mild-mannered clerk, or perhaps a bookkeeper.

The irony is that Rusty is on his way to Ramsay Airways. He's their top bush pilot. Not only that, he's thought to be the most experienced bush pilot in the world! He's logged over 33,000 hours in the 46 years he's been flying planes into the northern wilderness.

He doesn't fit the image of those early swashbuckling, adventurous men who flew into rugged bush country, putting down their small planes into small spaces. But he's one of the pioneers in the business and he knows Northern Ontario like the back of his hand.

He began his career in 1937 with Austin Airways as a general helper. The next year he became a pilot and has been ferrying freight and passengers to Indian reserves, mining settlements and isolated outposts ever since.

To the sick, lost or injured in a cruel country that shows no pity, Rusty's mercy missions have often made the difference between life and death. But he's modest and unassuming. He plays down his exploits and attributes the fact that he's never had a serious accident to "common sense, but mostly luck."

Rusty took my wife Jenny and me for a short trip over the Sudbury area. I asked him about the mystique surrounding the rough-and-ready daring of the pilots of fiction. He dismissed the idea as the product of overly active imaginations.

"We had some characters, all right," he said with a grin. "But all of them were dedicated pilots."

As we landed on Lake Ramsay after our run with the famous airman, Jenny said, "If I'd been holding a full cup of coffee, I wouldn't have spilled a drop."

Rusty's age is a well-kept secret, but his friends say he must be in his mid-seventies. He'll likely hit the half-century mark as a bush pilot!

Canada's Coldest Spot

At White River, north of Sault Ste. Marie, there's a big, broken thermometer a few yards off the Trans Canada Highway that reads 72 degrees below zero.

It commemorates the memorable day back in 1935 when a record breaking low was established, and White River was proclaimed The Coldest Spot in Canada!

We stayed there overnight a few times while travelling Northern Ontario. At White River, people don't even bother to talk about the cold unless it goes down to around minus 40 degrees. That might rate a casual comment.

During a cold snap one January when Torontonians shivered in a bone-chilling minus 29, it went down to 58 below in White River!

The villagers regard visitors - especially city slickers - in a somewhat condescending way, with a degree of pity. And there's no question they feel a certain pride, a certain superiority about their ability to cope with the cold. In fact, they seem to revel in really cold temperatures. But after all, it was the cold that put the place on the map.

I was lucky enough to meet an expert on cold at a little store called "The Trading Post." A grizzled old lumberman and trapper named Henry Duplessis - short, wiry and tough as nails. He's lived and worked in the area all his life and was in the bush the day when it went down to 72 below. He was with a crew and they kept right on working. They were building an ice road for sledding lumber and Henry said it was an ideal day for it.

He was telling me that city people feel the cold because they don't know how to dress for it. They don't wear wool underwear, the right footwear, pants and parkas.

Henry said he went down to Toronto during the winter to attend a wedding and just about froze to death because he had to wear "a monkey suit" for the wedding.

Since I was on a northern swing, I was wearing what I regard as heavy clothing. So I asked Henry if he thought I was properly dressed for the northern winter.

He told me I wouldn't survive in the bush for an hour. My sheepskin gloves were no good. I needed moose hide mitts with feathered lining - like his. And my boots? He just shook his head slowly.

"Son," said Henry, "If I took you out in the bush on my trapline, I'd be lugging you back in no time with frozen feet."

That's the way it is in White River. When I left the next morning, it was a balmy 20 below.

Staking a Claim

I am now a prospector. A mining man. And I have a prospector's licence to prove it. I have even staked a claim in the goldfields of Kirkland Lake!

The whole thing started when my wife Jenny, cameraman David Perrault and I went to Kirkland Lake to do a few stories about mining. While there we met Alex Peron, one of the many prospectors, engineers and geologists who frequent the Bon Aire Motel's coffee shop for breakfast.

Alex suggested we come back sometime and he'd show us how to stake a claim. He and his partner, Big John Duncan, have been prospecting the district for years and have staked more claims than you can shake a stake at.

Jenny and I talked about it during the winter and one beautiful

Bill, Jenny, Mary, Big John and Alex (kneeling) posing for a group shot the way prospectors of yesteryear used to do.
photo by: Northern News Photo

spring day we decided the time was ripe to go up to the goldfields to make our fortune.

So we packed our bags, took the Mustang and headed north. Spring was busting out all over. The northland was magnificent. We were to go into the bush the next day. Alex and Big John expected us. David was flying up from the city.

But the next day the roof fell in. It was snowing, blowing and cold. David's plane was delayed. He arrived about noon, undaunted by the weather. He said it would lend an authentic note and he'd get some great pictures.

I put on a bold front and told Alex and Big John that after all I'd been to places like Greenland and Yellowknife and the weather wouldn't bother me a bit.

Jenny, who has never been considered a golddigger, was rarin' to go on this jaunt. She hopped in a panel truck with Mary Greer, a geological technician who works with Duncan and Peron and Steve Rayment, a reporter from the "Northern News", who was doing a story on us.

We drove over to the recording office. I got my prospectors' licence and a map of the Boston Creek area, along with metal claim tags. An hour later we were on the edge of the bush, ready to go in and restake a 6-acre claim.

I sensed that this was the beginning of a new career. I felt I was on the verge of a great discovery. I would become a mining magnate. I hadn't been this close to a fortune since I once blew the bundle and bought a Wintario ticket.

We trudged through the snow into the bush. I had an axe to blaze the claim trail. Big John cut down a tree with a few easy swipes. Alex squared off a claim stake. I nailed on a metal tag. David recorded the epic trek on tape.

We forged ahead. My hands were cold. My feet were cold. My bones chilled to the marrow. We found an abandoned cabin. I huddled there shivering in silence. Then we moved on.

As we left, and I followed Big John's footsteps through the snow, I began to think that prospectors earn their money. On the other hand, the stakes are high.

So I'll be back there again to claim my fortune. Count on it! Maybe this year, or maybe next year. Or maybe the year after that.

James Bay Frontier

Northern Ontario has a style, a certain character of its own. It's hard to put your finger on it. I'm drawn to its rugged terrain, the vast forests, the lakes and streams, the pure white snow in winter, the tracks of moose by the roadside.

But it's more than that. It's the people. They're warm and direct. They're proud of the northland, of the scenery, of the wild life, of their towns and villages, and of their heritage.

They're even proud of their sub-zero temperatures. We were driving up to Cochrane for the annual Snow Carnival which is always held in the second week of February. We took a coffee break at Iroquois Falls. It was 25 below at the time.

I mentioned the cold temperatures to an older man sitting nearby. He had a weather-beaten face and was obviously a woodsman or a prospector, or something like that.

"It's a bit nippy," he growled. "But in 1935, it went to 79 below here one day. It's in the Guiness Book of Records."

We mushed on to Cochrane where I renewed acquaintance with Mayor Ray Fortier. I had met him when we went to Greenland for the Timmins-Greenland Games. Albert Boisvert was with Ray. He's a retired Cochrane industrialist, and a dead-ringer for George Burns. Albert was also on the Greenland trip. Ruth Burkholder showed up. She and her buddies had organized the Games.

We talked about the weather in Greenland. It hadn't gone more

Cochrane Carnival "Chief", Bill and cameraman Jim McDonald. It was 25° below at the time.
photo by: J. Bramah

than 20 below when we were there. But even as we talked it had slid to 39 below in Cochrane!

That didn't bother the Carnival Committee a bit. Everything went off as planned. Cameraman Jim MacDonald arrived by plane and we began shooting. We had plenty to work with. We started with Chimo, the giant polar bear at the entrance to the town, and got shots of the famed Polar Bear Express as it pulled in from Moosonee.

The Carnival was billed as Ontario's biggest. And I can believe it. The hotels were booked solid and everything else was frozen solid. We watched snow sculpture being carved with chain saws.

On Lake Commando, in the centre of town, there was a dog pull, log sawing and the pulp throw. We met the Snow Queen and her court and saw talented figure skaters at the Tim Horton Arena.

When Albert, who's in his seventies plunged into icy waters for the Polar Bear Dip, I became convinced that the North was the home of the brave!

But the most spectacular event of all was the children's torchlight parade that wound through the streets to a huge bonfire at the lake. Then fireworks added additional northern lights to the sky.

By the time we left, it had gone up to 10 below. The mayor admitted it had been a 'cold snap.' We wouldn't have wanted it any other way. It was the northland at its vigorous best. The way it's supposed to be on the James Bay frontier.

Canada's Largest City

Did you know that Timmins is Canada's largest city? It sprawls for 1,200 miles through forests, lakes and streams. You could put Toronto, Montreal, New York and Winnipeg in it and still have room for a few more towns and villages. The populated part of the city of 45,000 is quite modern. It has big shopping plazas and all that sort of thing.

Quite a change from the days when I began my broadcasting career up there over 35 years ago working for Roy Thomson. The "Timmins Press" was the newspaper magnate's first venture into publishing and station CKGB one of his first radio stations.

Timmins has been thought of as a city of gold since the early 1900's when prospectors like Sandy McIntyre, Hollinger and others discovered glamorous gold - rugged pioneers who put a little town on the map.

When I lived and worked there, gold was still the major industry. I remember doing a story about going down in the McIntyre mine. But when I revisited Timmins after all those years, I saw something I'd never seen before. I saw gold being poured!

The City of Timmins and the Pamour people, who now own McIntyre, arranged the visit.

When we arrived, we were led to an old brick building. A seal was broken on a heavy door and we entered a room that glittered from the reflection of the furnaces. Armed guards were standing around. Gold spewed from the furnaces into moulds. The slag was scraped away, the gold was removed, cleaned, drilled, stamped and weighed.

Those gold bricks are heavy. They look very much like an ordinary brick, except for the colour. But they weigh about 65 pounds. For a brief moment, I held bar number 13,361 from the famed McIntyre in my arms. It's unlikely we'll ever meet again!

Gold is no longer the big metal in Timmins. It's been replaced by copper and zinc.

But as I was telling Yves St. Jacques, the great guy who showed us around, I'll always think of Timmins as the city with a heart of gold!

Old Mountie

We met Bill Oram while on a swing through Northwestern Ontario. Now crowding 90, he's thought to be one of the last surviving members of the Royal Northwest Mounted Police. That's what the world-famous force was called before it became the R.C.M.P.

We had a hard time tracking him down. He lives on a side street in Thunder Bay with his pet pigeon "Chick" who perches on his shoulder and seems to have the run of Oram's bungalow.

Jenny and I along with Global cameraman Jim MacDonald, spent a morning with the active old Mountie and came away with enough stories to shoot a documentary if we'd wanted to.

Corporal Bill Oram joined the R.N.W.M.P. in 1919. He has pictures showing him on his horse "Spider" and he looks very much like the typical Mountie you see on travel folders. Another old photo shows him in the bush on snowshoes.

Although the blood and thunder angles about the force played up in novels and films have been overdone, some of the glamorous exploits did occur occasionally.

Corporal Bill recalls being sent up the B.C. coast to track a man charged with killing his wife. He found the woman's body in a burned out car that had been run into a gully and finally got his man in mountainous country, miles from the scene of the crime.

On another occasion, he prevented a possible murder when he disarmed a burly woodsman wielding a knife at a dance hall in Nipigon.

He says one of the most interesting assignments was in 1921 when he was a security man during a visit to Canada by the Prince of Wales, later Edward VIII. In later years, when the present Queen was touring Canada, she asked to meet this Corporal who had guarded her uncle.

Corporal Oram served mostly in the West, but as the force moved eastward, he was stationed in Fort William, now Thunder Bay.

When he retired, he decided to stay there. He has a few good friends and plenty of memories. But he can't recall ever meeting a mountie who rode off into the sunset singing "Rose Marie."

Timmins-Greenland Games

We went to Greenland and had a whale of a time covering the Timmins-Greenland Winter Games.

It was an off-beat assignment. For several years, top-flight athletes from Timmins and Greenland had been meeting in a sports and cultural exchange. The games were held in Timmins in 1982. In 1983, 48 of the athletes flew by charter plane to the city of Nuuk in Southern Greenland.

Since I cover Ontario, Global thought it would be a good idea for me to go along. My wife, Jenny, who is my production assistant and ordinarily travels with us, would have no part of it.

"There's no way I'm going up there and freeze to death for a week," she muttered. She stayed home and packed in some games with her bridge buddies.

So cameraman Terry Culbert and I flew from Toronto to Timmins, stayed overnight and flew to Greenland the next morning on an Austin Airways plane to Nuuk. It took us ten hours, with refueling stops at Whale Island and Frobisher Bay.

It was an unforgettable experience. Both Terry and I have done a fair bit of travelling, but Greenland is in a class by itself for splendour in scenery. All of us on the plane were shocked into silence when we got our first glimpse of the towering icecaps. They were intimidating, even frightening in their remote, awesome beauty.

We landed at Nuuk airport and took a cab into the city through what seemed to be almost a tunnel of ice and snow. The population of Nuuk is only 10,000 but they still call it a city. And it looks like one.

There are urban style apartments, occupied by mostly Inuit families and many small, colourful houses. There's a shopping centre and shops scattered around where you can buy just about everything. It's all imported. Greenland's only major industry is fishing.

Denmark colonized Greenland two centuries ago, and has poured millions of kroners into it ever since. Although there are only 9,000 Danes of a total population of about 49,000, their influence is everywhere. Greenland got Home Rule in 1981 and the new premier is an Inuit. He was telling us he hopes to reconstruct things so that Eskimo culture will not die completely.

The next day we went by helicopter over the infamous "Iceberg Alley" to an Eskimo village. There were tidy cottages throughout the village. Not an igloo in sight. Not even a spear. Inuit now use fishing vessels and send their catch to the modern processing plants along the coast.

The following day we covered the games. There were Alpine and Nordic skiing, indoor soccer, badminton and karate. Greenlanders know nothing about hockey or curling. In the overall picture,

Timmins edged Greenland slightly, I think. Nobody seemed too clear about it. But everybody won on the friendship front.

And was it cold? You can bet your last Eskimo pie on it. Oldtimers said it was Greenland's coldest winter in 100 years!

Bill and cameraman Terry Culbert at Nuuk, the capital of Greenland. It was the coldest winter in 100 years.

Beardmore Relics

Have you ever heard of the Beardmore relics? They used to be mentioned in grade six history books as proof that the Vikings reached the Beardmore area of Northwestern Ontario over 1,000 years ago. Kids don't read about them anymore. And for good reason. The relics were a hoax.

The yarn began in a little museum up at Lakehead and ended at Toronto's prestigious ROM - the Royal Ontario Museum.

It started innocently enough. I was travelling the north shore of Lake Superior and dropped in to take a look at the museum in the town of Nipigon.

"Buzz" Lein, the museum's founder, was there. He's not exactly the type you expect to find in a museum. A big, burly guy - tough, irascible, with a rasping voice you can hear all over the little building.

It turned out that, aside from being a history buff, he had been a logger in the area for 44 years before he retired, and knew the district like the back of his hand. Before I had a chance to take a look at the place, he collared me to see if I'd help him uncover the Beardmore Relics! Bring them out in the open!

"Buzz" was vehement...he said the relics were supposed to be at the ROM. But for years he'd been trying to get them to Nipigon for temporary display and had been getting nowhere. He clutched a thick file of correspondence of what he called "bureaucratic gobble-de-gook." Scads of letters from the ROM - all evading the issue. Buzz suspected the Relics had been lost!

Mary Gordon, editor of the "Nipigon Gazette," came in. She'd been reporting the running battle for five years. She told me that one Spring the MPP for the District, Jack Stokes, had joined in the fray, but he too had been caught in the bureaucratic stranglehold.

I went over to the newspaper office and went through Mary's file. Finally, I go the drift of the story.

Back in the thirties, a gold prospector named Jimmy Dodd managed to get his hands on an authentic Viking sword about a thousand years old. He took it down to Toronto and convinced senior ROM archeologists that he'd found it in the bush in the Beardmore area. It was authentic. It looked like quite a find. They bought it.

Later, it was learned that Jimmy Dodd had stolen it from a Nipigon boarding home. How it got there, nobody knows.

I phoned the ROM and, sure enough, was shuffled from one source to another. People were evasive. I began to see the humour in the whole thing. The mighty ROM was embarrassed!

I kept in touch and eventually talked to Elizabeth Stevens, a bright authoritative staffer who agreed that the real value of the relics was in the folklore involved. That's what "Buzz" had maintained all along.

The ROM didn't want to perpetuate a hoax, and had hoped to sweep it all under the rug. To their credit, they relented.

Later at the ROM, I watched conservator Christopher Toogood making reproductions of the pieces of an ancient Viking sword -the Beardmore Relics! When completed, they'd be taken back to the North Shore of Lake Superior - to the little Nipigon museum.

I phoned "Buzz" to tell him the news. He howled with glee! He was elated! Grateful words kept tumbling out and I'll bet they could hear those rasping shouts over on Nipigon's main street.

The Dionnes Today

There's a little house on the highway on the outskirts of North Bay. It's the original Dionne farmhouse, now a museum, and I went back to see it on the 50th anniversary of a birth that made medical history.

About 4 a.m. on May 28, 1934, the Dionne Quintuplets made their dramatic entrance into this world.

Even if you weren't around when the event occurred, the odds are that you're as familiar with their existence as you are with Niagara Falls, Mount Everest or Queen Victoria.

Even the country doctor, Dr. Alan Dafoe, who delivered the last three babies, didn't expect them to survive more than a few hours. Their combined weight was only 13 lbs. 5 oz.

The infants were placed in a butcher's basket, the only thing available to hold them. The doctor put the basket beside an old wood stove in the kitchen to keep the tiny babies warm, and turned his attention to the mother, Mrs. Elzira Dionne, who already had a family of five children. Oliva Dionne, the father, was in an understandable state of shock!

When the babies continued to live, the impact struck — history was in the making!

Press people from everywhere converged on the farmhouse, originally located midway between the villages of Callender and Corbeil in the North Bay area. Promoters sped to the scene, trying to get Papa Dionne to sign contracts for everything from circus appearances to endorsement of soaps. Presents, five of each, came from all over the world.

For a few months, the Quints lived with their family in the farmhouse, which during the depths of the Depression had neither electricity nor running water. But they had become "the world's darlings." Everyone felt they should have the best of everything. They were taken from their family by the Ontario Government, declared wards of the State and a trust fund was set up for them. A special nursery with a glassed-in playground for public observation was erected across from their home. For nine years they attended functions, endorsed products and up to 3,000 people a day would visit them.

I recall going to see them. It was like a carnival. There were concession booths everywhere. Everyone made money from the Quints, including their parents, relatives, Dr. Dafoe, even the midwives.

The life-in-a-fishbowl proved tragic for the Quints. Papa Dionne went to court and won his daughters back, taking them to live in an 18-room mansion he had built. He surrounded it with barbed wire. But it was too late. The Quints couldn't get along with their family and eventually moved to the Montreal area.

Today, only three survive. Emilie, an epileptic, died at the age of

19, and Marie died at 36 of a heart attack. The others live in St. Bruno, a Montreal suburb. Annette and Cecile are both separated from their husbands. Yvonne tried unsuccessfully to become a nun. Mrs. Dionne is an invalid. Oliva died in 1979.

About 30,000 people still visit the Quints' Museum. Some to recall the days when the story was unfolding, others to learn of the famous five and the childhood that was never their own.

Science North

The good news from Sudbury on June 19, 1984 was the opening of Science North. If you get a chance to visit it, you'll find out it's not just any old science centre. Science North is a knockout!

The major part of the complex consists of two big buildings which from the air look like snowflakes resting on a giant rock. It's a deliberate design symbolic of the glaciers that shaped the country.

The main building is set on a huge rock cavern, a reminder of the meteorite impact two billion years ago that created the Sudbury basin, and the entrance can only be described as simply spectacular!

You go in through a wide tunnel of rock leading to a magnificent amphitheatre with walls of massive rock formations. There you can pause to watch a 3-D film that has brought rave reviews from critics, then go to a vast spiral ramp that winds upward and upward, taking you to the exhibit floors.

The exhibits range from a world seismographic station to artisans carving figures from soapstone.

"There's a lot of 'gee whiz' science around, and a tendency toward trivialization," says director Dr. David Pearson. "We're more interested in showing the real interests of science rather than gadgets."

You may remember the old Big Nickel Mine on the outskirts of the town. As a miniature mine, it was a somewhat dismal tourist attraction. But Science North took it over, refurbished it and made it an exciting part of the whole operation.

The little mine has become a real showplace. It's always been Ontario's only hard rock mine that's open to the public. But now you see a very accurate small-scale version of what goes on down in the big fellas.

You are taken down to watch miners actually drilling and blasting and there's even a model of Inco's experimental underground garden. I've been down in the real one, which is over 5,000 feet below the surface and some years ago, had the honour of picking the first tomato off the vines.

While barnstorming through the north as a young newsman, I lived in Sudbury for a year or so, and in recent years have seen it change from a rather hard-boiled mining town to a well-rounded city both commercially and culturally.

Science North is the icing on the cake.

Sudbury's Science North is an eye-opener. The buildings were designed to look like snowflakes.

Highway Book Shop

Ordinarily you wouldn't expect a new and used book store to be a tourist attraction. But the Highway Book Shop in the Cobalt area is no ordinary bookstore.

First of all, it's out in the middle of nowhere. There's nothing but bush country around it. It's miles from any urban centre. There are just a few farm houses in the distance. And the only apparent signs of activity are the cars and trucks on nearby Highway 11 which leads up to the James Bay Frontier.

But the Highway Book Shop startles people who stop there. Because it's huge! Although it's way out in the country, it's vast! It rambles on and on. And there are over a quarter of a million books on the shelves!

Every time I've visited the big complex there have been several people wandering around looking at, or buying, books. During the summer the big store is visited by an average of 1,000 buyers or browsers a week.

In the back part of the building is the publishing side of the business. In terms of titles produced, the Highway Book Shop ranks up there with Ontario's top publishers. The last I heard they'd published over 200 titles, the majority small books about the north country.

The man behind this success story is Doug Pollard. In 1957 he and his wife opened a small printing shop on some property they owned beside Highway 11. Later they began to sell books as a sideline. Then people started to ask for more local historical materials, and Pollard began printing local pamphlets. Eventually he branched out into publishing northern authors.

The whole thing mushroomed and there are now 12 full time employees. The walls bulge with books. The presses are constantly printing and reprinting publications.

Pollard himself is a book addict. A voracious reader. And he's been a boon to writers and artists who live in the northland. He's so highly regarded that Nipissing University conferred an honorary Doctor of Letters degree upon him, because of his contribution to culture in the north.

I've never met Dr. Pollard. He's on the road much of the time buying books, arranging distribution and so forth. I've heard about him, read about him, and seen pictures of him, but locating him has always eluded me. Of course, I'm always travelling too.

A publisher friend of mine, Ian Rhind, tried for months to arrange a meeting of Doug and myself. One time we were close, but missed each other by about five minutes.

I hope our paths cross someday. Hopefully, right on his home ground. At Ontario's now-famous Book Shop.

How To Get There

Southwestern Ontario

Ontario's Main Street/9   Ontario's main street — for better or for worse. Needs no introduction.

Punkydoodles Corner/11   This can be tricky. If you're coming from Toronto take the 401 to exit 35. Head for Stratford on Highways 7 and 8. When you come to New Hamburg, keep on going to Waterloo Regional Road 1 and 22. Go south 7½ miles and you'll hit Punkydoodles. On Harvey Meuller's front lawn you'll see a sign saying "Mayor's House". Harvey will be glad to show you the town. You can see it all from his front porch.

Garden of Weeds/12   Look for the Botany Building. The Administration office or one of the students around the campus will direct you. The garden is near the building. There's a small hothouse beside it. The weeds are at the peak of their beauty late in the summer.

Granny's Duvets/13   Downcraft is located at 2202 Jerseyville Road West. It's two miles west of Highway 52, which is west of Hamilton.

World's Champion Birdwatcher/14   Wheatley is on most road maps. It's near Leamington on Lake Erie. Everybody knows Norman. If you're a serious birder he'll be glad to talk to you. Phone first. He's often off on jaunts to various parts of the world.

Elora's Power Play/15   Elora is in the Guelph area, easily found on a road map. The Elora Mill is down at the end of Mill St. which you will see when you enter the village.

Old Buggies/16   There are only two buggy makers in Ontario. Both are Old Order Mennonites and prefer to remain anonymous. However, if you're a serious buyer, go to Elmira and ask one of the black-garbed Mennonites for the location. You'll see Mennonites around Elmira and nearby St. Jacobs. They are friendly people, and if convinced of your sincerity will likely direct you to one or both of the buggy shops.

The Donnellys Today/18

It's on Highway 7, north of London. Lucan is on most road maps. You can see where the Donnellys are buried, visit the church, and if you're lucky, meet Father Finn.

Sled Dogs/19

Tom and his wife can usually be found at the Monument Company just off the main street. Chesley is southwest of Owen Sound and easy to find on most maps.

The Sky's the Limit/20

Go north off 401 at Kitchener at exit 34. Go about ½ mile for the Doon turn-off. Go past the General Store and you'll see a small sign on the left saying "Fantasy Promotions".

Ontario Peanuts/22

On Highway 24 a few miles north of Simcoe. It's a big blue building right by the highway. They're happy to show you around and you'll find out everything you always wanted to know about peanuts.

Turkey Talk/23

Hybrid is in Kitchener. Better phone first if you want to see the giant turkeys. The turkey story we did on TV was a giant spoof, and later was on Steve Allen's "Most Embarrassing Moments" on ABC in the States.

Fishing Village/24

Port Dover is on Lake Erie south of Brantford. It's a village with a style all of its own.

Kipp's Garage/25

Aylmer is one of the towns in Southwestern Ontario where the big canning factories are located. Jerry's name is in the phone book. He's in and out.

The Slow-Pokes/26	Call Vic in Burford of Elsie Murphy in Port Dover for information. But don't rush them.
Blueberry Patches/28	The Weber's big farm is on the outskirts of St. Williams, south of Tillsonburg. To get to Powell's Patch, follow Highway 24 south from Simcoe to Radical Road. Go east on Radical Road about a mile or so and you'll see the sign. The Powell family also has a trained pet duck.
Ides of March/29	The Stratford Festival Theatre is considered one of the best of its kind on the continent. Signs on Highway 401 will direct you to it.
Butler's Farm Animals/30	Take 401 to exit 29 at Woodstock. Go south on Highway 59 a few hundred yards. You'll see Morrison's Body Shop. There's a lane beside it. Turn right, follow the lane to the barn. Say hello to Ross for me.
Cobblestone Houses/32	Paris is north of Brantford. It's a beautiful town. Go to the newspaper office on the main street. They'll be able to tell you where to find Margaret. She's well informed about the houses and their locations.
Tintinnabulator/33	Take 401 to Highway 6. Go south of Highway 5 to Clappison's Corners. Go east to Waterdown. Go through the town over the bridge. At top of the hill turn left at the first street. It's a short block. Turn left again to 29 James Street. Phone first.
Lombardo Legend/34	Go north on Springbank Road. About 100 yards south of the Guy Lombardo Bridge you'll see the museum.
Talking Earth Pottery/36	You'll like the Smith's place. Take the Cockshutt Road going south from Beautford. Go to Soursprings Road. Turn left. About a mile down the road you'll see the sign directing you to the cabin.
Kissing Bridge/38	West Montrose is in the Guelph area and

easy to locate on road maps. The general store was selling beautiful handmade crafts the last time I was there.

Youngest Postmaster/39   Harley is snuggled into the countryside south of Brantford. Take Highway 24 south to the Brantford Airport. Go west on Highway 53 to Burford. There, take County Road 2 to Harley. The unusual post office is behind the general store. The postmaster was thinking of going to university when I saw him, but I'm sure Grandpa will still be there.

Backus Mill/41   Look for Port Rowan on a road map. It's one of the fishing villages on Lake Erie's shoreline south of Tillsonburg. The Backus Mill area is just north of the village.

First Oil Well/42   Petrolia is a great little town. Be sure to visit "The Petrolia Discovery". It's an outdoor museum showing the history of commercial drilling. They can fill you in on all the details.

Old Streetcars/43   Take 401 to the Guelph Line. Go north to 25th sideroad. The Railway is just north of it.

"Doc" McKibbin/45   Lives on the outskirts of Wheatley. It's the same village where birdwatcher Norman Chesterfield lives. Wheatley has two internationally known personalities.

Fall Fairs/46   If you're from out of the province try to visit one. You'll sense the spirit of rural Ontario.

Oldest Pilot/47   You may meet Dick if he's around the club.

Forge and Anvil/49   You'll find St. Jacobs a few miles north of Waterloo on your road map. There are two or three ways to get there. The most direct is to go north from 401 at exit 34. Go through Kitchener and Waterloo. The village is just off Highway 85 which runs north from Waterloo.

Eastern and Central Ontario

Boldt Castle/51	You'll enjoy the boat trip from Gananoque through some of the Thousand Islands to the castle. Gananoque, by the way, is east of Kingston and a short distance south of the 401.
Birdhouse City/53	Located south of Belleville, Picton is one of the most historic and picturesque places in the province. Somebody at the Conservation Centre will show you around.
The Philoxians/54	Take Highway 41 north from Napanee. After you go through Roblin keep watching for the county road on the left which takes you to Marlbank. The Philoxians are located on the outskirts. The villagers are very proud of the Philoxians. Anyone will direct you to their location.
The Magnetic Hill/55	Dacre (people pronounce it da-ker) is in the Renfrew area. Take Highway 132 south. As I recall the Magnetic Hill is just a short distance west of the village. You'll see a highway department building on one side of the road. The hill is on the opposite side.
Windmill Man/56	Take Highway 33 west from Picton. Wellington isn't very big. Jerry's workshop is about ½ mile from the main street. Everyone knows him on the main street.
Fence Viewers/58	Check in your municipality. Your town clerk's office should have some information.
The Painting Priest/59	The icons are well worth seeing. Phone the church in Welland. I'm sure they'd tell you when the church is open and how to get to it.
Cactus Grower/60	Dundas is a bustling town west of Hamilton. Any resident or merchant will direct you to Ben's big greenhouse.

Rendezvous for Seniors/61	If you're a senior be sure to drop in during the summer. Harbourfront is a big complex at the foot of Toronto's Bay Street.
Rockhounds/62	You might like to drop in to one of the rock shops. "Winnie's" is the most visible. They'll tell you how to get to Paul's mine. In the Sword Motel's coffee shop they have a picture of me at the booth where I work when in Bancroft. It's one of my "offices" around the province.
Joey the Beaver/64	Look for Joey at outdoor shows. He'll be the beaver the children are patting.
Holland Marsh/65	If you'd like to meet Matt, turn off Highway 400 at Canal Road which takes you to the Muck Station. The office will direct you to Ansnorveldt.
Esmond's Tea Room/66	From Bancroft take Highway 62 north to Maynooth. It's about 12 miles from Bancroft. At Maynooth turn left on Highway 127. Go to Lake St. Peter Centre Road. You'll see Algonquin Lodge there. Turn right, Esmond's is on the north side about ¼ mile down the road. As I recall there are a couple of Lake St. Peter roads. Make sure you turn at the one mentioned above.
Monastery Row/68	The one to visit if you just want to get away from it all is the Cistercians. From Highway 400 take Highway 9 west to Airport Road. Go north a few miles and you'll see the sign directing you to their location.
Ice Fishing/69	From 401 take Highway 48 north to Beaverton which is on Lake Simcoe. There are several fish hut operations in the area. All of them know the lake like the back of their hands.
Pirate Ship/70	Take Highway 48 north from 401 to Sutton. Take Highway 9 to Jackson's Point which is on Lake Simcoe. Ask someone where the pirate ship is docked. The

	captain looks like a real pirate with a black beard and everything.
Dream Come True/72	Check with the Simcoe Fire Department as to when they are having their next meet.
Raising Crickets/73	The old warehouse is located near the Mohawk Chapel. You'd better phone first. They'll give you specific directions. Don't ask for their feeding formula. It's a secret.
Dollhouse Gallery/75	It's about a mile north of the Peace Bridge. Bertie Hall is a red brick building on the corner of Niagra Blvd. and Phitts.
Mr. Kite/76	Ken is in and out of his "studio". The best way to find him is to check with Ontario Place in Toronto. They'll tell you where he's appearing.
Ginseng Farm/78	You can see the farm from Highway 400 about 10 miles north of Metro Toronto. Take one of the nearby exits and double back if you want to get a closer look.
19th Century Man/79	Take Highway 400 and go west on Highway 9. You'll see the turn-off to Tottenham. Keep going a couple of miles on Highway 9 and you'll see York County Gun Works on the right side of the highway.
Last Duel Park/80	Perth is in the Ottawa Valley. I believe there is just one park in the town. I remember standing there one murky morning and reading the inscription on the gravestone before the actors began the duel.
Herb Homestead/82	Take 400 north to Highway 52. Go east and follow signs to Kettleby. It's a beautiful little hamlet. Ask at the General Store for the location of the Herb Homestead.
Clock Auction/83	You'll have to be an early bird for this one. Check in the phone book or through Directory Assistance for The Ontario

Flower Growers Association in Mississauga. They'll give you the days the auctions are being held.

Buggy Man/84

To get to Crown Hill take Highway 400 to Highway 11 which is a few miles north of Barrie. Go north to 93 and watch for Cedar Rail Farms. Bill welcomes tourists. He has one of the best collections of buggies on the continent which he has restored himself.

School Patrollers/86

From 401 go north on Oshawa's Simcoe Street. You go right through the city. You'll see Durham College on the left and the entrance to the camp on the right. It's a huge place. A piece of Muskoka-type country right in an industrial city.

World's Champion Songwriter/87

George will be delighted to see you. From 401 take 400 north to Highway 9, then west to Airport Road. Go north to Hockley Valley Road. Go east about a mile. George's place is on the right. His phone number is in the Orangeville directory. He's often travelling so it might be wise to phone first.

Taj Mahal/88

Take Highway 48 to Ringwood. Cut across to Stouffville on Highway 14. Then take 47 to Uxbridge. The exotic building is a short distance from the town. The Foster Memorial is open one Sunday a month, I believe. For further information call the public relations people at the Canada Permanent Trust Company, which handles the estate.

Toymaker/90

From 401 take Highway 48 north to Ringwood. Go east to Stouffville. Paul's Place is on the east side of the village.

Little Red Schoolhouse/91

The best way to visit the school is to call the Peel Board of Education. You'll have to do as you're told or Mr. Potter will slap a dunce cap on you!

Peterborough Postcard Company/93	From 401 take Highway 115 north to Peterborough. You'll go in on The Queensway. Turn right at the end of The Queensway. You'll be on Erskine. Look for Cameron. Harry's Peterborough Postcard Company is at 456 Cameron. If you get mixed up, go to Artspace in the Market Hall under the town clock. They know Harry. Artspace itself is worth a visit.
The Forgotten Chapel/94	Deseronto is east of Belleville. From Deseronto take Highway 2 to the Tyendinaga Reserve. Ask someone where Father Ken lives. He'll be glad to open the chapel for you and tell you plenty of historical tidbits.
Merry-Go-Round/95	Lakeside Park is at Port Dalhousie, now part of St. Catharines. Follow the signs or better still ask one of the storekeepers or residents where the park is located. I watched part of the restoration. It was truly a labour of love.
Len Cullen — Dreamer/96	Take 401 to Highway 12 at Whitby. Go north a few miles to Taunton Road. Turn left and go about half a mile. You will see it on the right.
Barn Raising/98	From Toronto take Highway 404 to Highway 8 to Vandorf. There's a museum on the left. The barn is behind the museum.

Muskoka and Southern Georgian Bay

Roughing It/100	Killarney Park is ruggedly beautiful. Take Highway 69 from Parry Sound. Turn left at Highway 627 which takes you right in.
Backstage at Ste. Marie/102	If you've never been to Ste. Marie among the Hurons in Midland, you'll be impressed. They'll tell you where the behind-the-scenes people are located if you're interested. The children with me in the pic-

ture on the book's cover were at Ste. Marie for what's call a winter "live-in". It's a three day-and-night experience, living as pioneers.

Birdman of Bala/103   Jim lives a few doors south of the O.P.P. offices. You'll see the pigeon loft in the backyard of his house.

Scoots/104   Unless you're with an experienced guide it's not wise to go looking for scoots in the area where my friend McKinnon took me. You might see the odd scoot around the Parry Sound dock or around the Midland-Penetang area.

Canada's Purest Water/106   This one is right in my own backyard. When I go up to our farm, I take 400 to the Hillsdale cut-off at Highway 93. Stay on 93 until you come to the four corners in Penetanguishene. Take Robert Street west about a mile and you'll see the water works at Champlain Road. It's great water.

Cranberry Farm/107   Take 400 to Highway 69. You'll see the Gibson Reserve and Cranberry Farm signs on the east side of 69.

Marine Railway/108   Take 400 to Coldwater. Go north through the village to the sign directing you to Big Chute. There's a winding road and you finally come upon the massive structure.

Magic of Muskoka/109   The magic starts around Orillia and just goes on and on.

Red Baron/110   Take Highway 11 north to the Bracebridge area, near High Falls bridge. You'll see the turn-off to Utterson. Go past the General Store to Highway 141. Turn right. Go to Old Parry Sound Road. Go about 2 miles. Watch for Otto's mail box. If you get mixed up, ask someone. Everybody knows him.

Bygone Days Farm/112   There are several routes to Collingwood. Take Sixth Street out toward "the mountain". You'll see the farm on the right. But phone first. I believe it's listed under Fisher, rather than Bygone Days. Sunday is the best day to go. They're pretty busy during the week.

Old Organs/113 Take 400 and Highway 93 to Midland. The Nicholson's live on Hugel Avenue. But it's essential to phone first.

The Hidden Talents/114 Call Father Greg Humbert at the Church of the Good Shepherd in Espanola or write Box 610 to find out where and when the group is playing.

Steamer Clarke/116 In the summer, Steamer generally has a boat you can see down at the town dock.

Severn Bird Farm/117 Severn Bridge is north of Orillia on Highway 11. Keep your eyes peeled for the Bird Farm sign on the east side of the highway. The turn-off is Concession 12.

Missing the Boat/118 The tough craft are birthed at Midland, Port Colborne and so on. Don't plan on sailing with them. I was just lucky.

Two Turtles/120 On a good day you can hear Bill or Emmy. It's hard to tell one beep from another, of course.

Heat from Peat/121 You can get peat products at some stores in Parry Sound. There are peat bogs in the area, but you need an expert with you to spot them.

Maple Syrup/122 Take Highway 27 north from Barrie. Elmvale is about 15 miles north. As you enter the village you'll see a lumber company on the right. The road beside it is what I call Maple Syrup row. The three big bushes are Ken Ritchie's, the Lalonde's and the Greenlaw's.

Bud Watson Galley/124 As you enter Midland on Highway 93 you'll see shopping plazas on both sides of the street. Turn right at Hugel Ave. and keep going down the main street. The gallery in in the former YMCA building. It houses one of the finest displays you'll see anywhere in a privately owned gallery.

Bigwin Inn/126   On Bigwin Island near Huntsville. You'd have to hire a boat to get there.

Northern Ontario

Harry's Chateau/128   Take Highway 11 north to Highway 66 and go east to Kirkland Lake. The museum is on the left as you go into the town. Across the road is a big motel. It used to be the bunkhouse for Harry's miners. It also has a superb dining room.

Bush Pilot/130   Highway 69 takes you to Sudbury. Rusty works out of Ramsay Lake Airways. That's not too far from the Sheraton-Coswell Hotel where we stay when in the Nickel City. Phone first. Rusty is a busy pilot, but the sort of man who will always take time to greet you.

Canada's Coldest Spot/131   It's on the Trans Canada Highway —that's highway 17. You'll go through some beautiful country along Lake Superior's north shore. From the highway you can see the famous Canada Goose statue at Wawa as you travel toward White River where the big thermometer is prominently displayed.

Staking a Claim/132   Alex is often in the Bon Aire Motel coffee shop during the breakfast hour. It's a great place to meet rugged looking prospectors. When you're in Kirkland Lake be sure to take a look at Charlie's Hotel on the main street. It's about the same as it was in the old days.

James Bay Frontier/134	Highway 11 takes you to Cochrane. If you ever get a chance to attend the carnival, don't miss it.
Canada's Largest City/136	We get to Timmins at least once a year. That great guy, Yves St. Jacques, who's the captain with the fire department, always shows us around. Say hello to Yves for me if you happen to meet him.
Old Mountie/137	Phone first. He and "Chick" are a great team. He has lots of pictures of the early days of the world-famous "Mounties".
Timmins-Greenland Games/138	The last I heard Ruth Burkholder was trying to arrange another trip. This time to Iceland.
Beardmore Relics/140	Nipigon is about 60 miles east of Thunder Bay. Ask anyone in town where the museum is located.
The Dionnes/142	The Quints Museum is on Highway 11 on the southern outskirts of North Bay. It's open during the summer.
Science North/144	As you come into Sudbury on Highway 69 turn right on Paris Road and right again on University Road. That's it!
Highway Book Shop/146	On Highway 11 near Cobalt. There are highway signs leading to it. An incredible place! Maybe you'll have better luck meeting Doug than I've had.

More great books from Cannonbooks!

Ontario & Outdoors

Atlas of Ontario Ghost Towns and Backroads	by Ron Brown	$ 9.95
Ghost Towns of Ontario, Vol. 1	by Ron Brown	8.95
Ghost Towns of Ontario, Vol. 2	by Ron Brown	8.95
Bill Bramah's Ontario	by Bill Bramah	9.95
Great Lakes Shipwrecks and Survivals	by W. Rautigan	12.95
Long Blue Edge of Ontario	by Doris Scharfenberg	12.95
Trent-Severn Boaters Directory		6.95
Giants of Canada's Ottawa Valley	by Joan Finnigan	12.95
Wilderness Survival	by Berndt Berglund	5.95
Wilderness Harvest	by Berndt Berglund	3.95
Ports, Lake Ontario Cruising Guide		10.00
Ports, Georgian Bay Cruising Guide		12.95
Introducing Eastern Wildflowers	by E. Barrie Kavasch	3.50
Guide to Eastern Mushrooms	by E. Barrie Kavasch	4.95
Guide to Eastern Rocks & Minerals	by James W. Grandy	3.95

Cookbooks

The Complete Gas BBQ Cookbook	by Jo-Anne Bennett	$ 9.95
Fare for Friends		12.95
Bean Cuisine	by Nan Tupper Chapman	14.95
Easy, Elegant Entertaining	by Iris Sainty	8.95
The Fondue Cookbook		9.95
Wilderness Cooking	by Berndt Burglund	3.95
49 North Cooks Wild		11.95
Charcoal and Woodsmoke		11.95
My Very Own Cookbook		14.95

Sports, Humour & Health

NHL Official Guide and Record Book		$14.95
Tennis, A Humorous Dictionary	by Peter Jensen	5.95
Joy of Stress	by Dr. Peter Hanson	9.95

Buy them at your local bookstore or use this handy coupon for ordering

---

Cannonbooks, 25-2 Connell Ct., Toronto, Ont. M8Z 1E8

Please send me the books I have checked above. I am enclosing $_____ (please add $1.00/book to cover postage and handling) in the form of a cheque or money order. (no cash or C.O.D.'s please). Please allow 4 weeks for delivery.

Name: _____

Address: _____

_____ Postal Code: _____